A
TEACHER'S GUIDE
TO UNDERSTANDING THE
DISRUPTIVE BEHAVIOUR
DISORDERS

A
TEACHER'S GUIDE
TO UNDERSTANDING THE
DISRUPTIVE BEHAVIOUR
DISORDERS

Attention Deficit Hyperactivity Disorder, Oppositional Defiant Disorder, and Conduct Disorder

PEARNEL BELL

authorHOUSE®

AuthorHouse™
1663 Liberty Drive
Bloomington, IN 47403
www.authorhouse.com
Phone: 1-800-839-8640

Published by AuthorHouse   06/11/2013

ISBN: 978-1-4685-4013-0 (sc)
ISBN: 978-1-4685-4012-3 (e)

Library of Congress Control Number: 2012903422

Printed in the United States of America

DEDICATION

I dedicate this book to the memory of my mother, Melita Edmond, who believed that education was important and that all should strive to attain it.

ACKNOWLEDGEMENTS

The journey of writing this book was challenging because this is my first nonfiction book, and I wanted to ensure that I was producing a book that would be beneficial to the readers. It would not have been possible to accomplish this arduous task without the help of several persons. I must first thank the teachers and principals who responded with such enthusiasm and were instrumental in making the research a success.

I want to say thanks to my editor, at Author House, who provided valuable guidance in formatting and editing the information in a manner that is simple and understandable to readers. I want also to thank Dr. Daniel Eckstein for his valuable contribution in reviewing the book and providing feedback.

I want to thank my mother, though deceased, for instilling in me values of determination, hard work, perseverance, and diligence. It was the combination of these qualities in me and the help of all the aforementioned that made the completion of this book possible.

FOREWORD

It is with great pride and joy that I have decided to publish a book for teachers in helping them understand and deal with students who present with disruptive behaviour disorders. I have been a teacher for the past thirty-four years and take delight in teaching. The teaching/learning process can become quite challenging when teachers must contend with children with behavioural problems. It therefore necessitates that teachers understand disruptive behaviours so that they are able to develop effective strategies to deal with behavioural problems in the classroom.

The purpose of this book is to bring into awareness the need for teachers to understand that some of the problems that students face are real-life psychological disorders that often have a biological basis and not merely environmental factors contributing to the behavioural pattern. It is also important that teachers recognize that addressing behavioural problems in the classroom cannot be adequately dealt with by the teacher; but needs an ecosystems approach that involve parents and other personnel in order to help the child reach his/her potential.

I think this book, *"A Teacher's Guide to Understanding the Disruptive Behaviour Disorders"*, is a little gem because the Jamaican Ministry of Education recently launched a programme to promote positive disciplinary practices in schools. The concept of positive disciplinary practice is a disciplinary approach that avoids the use of punitive measures and emphasizes reinforcement of good behaviour while fading out bad behaviour. Positive disciplinary practices eliminate verbally or physically abusing a child. I believe that for too long many teachers have used unfocused methods in dealing with children with behavioural problems, which often exacerbates the problem. The children were suspended or expelled from school and the teacher was completely stressed from having to contend with behavioural problems on a daily basis. It is my hope that the content of this book will provide greater insight into the behavioural disorders and help teachers develop better understanding of how to manage students who present with these disorders. It is my hope that this book will be used in teachers' colleges throughout Jamaica as a text and guide that provides an understanding for teacher trainees on how to deal with disruptive children. Many new teachers reported having been shocked when they entered teaching, had to contend with disruptive students, and absolutely did not know how to deal with them, hence increasing their frustration. The not-so-new teachers and even teachers who have been in the profession for a long time experience frustration because many had no effective method of how to deal with children presenting with disruptive behaviours. This book provides insight to teachers to help them develop greater understanding of behavioural disorders so that they can implement behavioural strategies that will help students succeed and help to reduce teachers' stress that result from contending with disruptive students.

I have conducted numerous workshops in schools in Jamaica on this very topic of dealing with disruptive behaviours. It is my pleasure to present the workshop content in a book that teachers can have on hand to consult when faced with the challenges of dealing with disruptive behaviours. I hope that you will certainly find this book useful in dealing with disruptions in the classroom.

TABLE OF CONTENTS

DEDICATION V

ACKNOWLEDGEMENTS vii

FOREWORD ix

INTRODUCTION xv

CHAPTER 1 1
Understanding the Disruptive Behaviour Disorders 1
ADHD, ODD and CD: Defined 3
Attention Deficit Hyperactivity Disorder (ADHD) 3
Oppositional Defiant Disorder (ODD) 6
Conduct Disorder (CD) 7
Comorbid Behaviour Disorders 9
Teachers' Perceptions and Knowledge of Disruptive
Behaviour Disorders 10
Teachers' Experiences With and Attitudes towards ADHD,
ODD, and CD Students 11
Teachers' Reactions and Intervention Strategies 13
Conclusion 16

CHAPTER 2 18
Jamaican Teachers' Experiences With and Attitudes towards
ADHD, ODD and CD Students 18
Jamaican Teachers' Qualitative Responses about Disruptive
Disorders 33
Qualitative Responses on Strategies Teachers Use to
Deal with Disruptive Students 40

CHAPTER 3 48
    Understanding the Importance of Medication as a
    Treatment Option 48
        History of Psychopharmacology and ADHD 50
        Assessing the Efficacy of Psychotropics in the
            Treatment of ADHD 50
    Cultural View of Medication as the First Line Treatment
    for ADHD: Jamaican Context 53
    The Efficacy of Alternative Treatments 54
    Optimal Arousal Theory 55
    Why Teachers Need to Know about Medication 55
    Medication for Oppositional Defiant Disorder and
    Conduct Disorder 56
    Future Trends 57
    Summary 58

CHAPTER 4 60
    Strategies Teachers Can Use to Deal with ADHD, ODD,
    and CD Students 60
        Self-Reflection on the Part of the Teacher 64
        Reframing 65
    Behaviour Modification Techniques 66
        Assertive Discipline: Strategies to Help Students with
            CD and ODD 66
    Strategies that May Diminish Power Struggles in the
    Classroom 68
    The ADHD Student 70
    Classroom Accommodations 71
    Teacher-Centred Approaches 72
    Over Plan, Avoid Information Overload 75
    Reinforcement Strategies, Selecting Appropriate Consequences 75
    General Tips for Working with ADHD Children 77

CHAPTER 5 85
    Self-Care: Stress Management for Life Management 85
    Centring to Reduce Stress 86
    Stress Management Tips for Life Management 88
    Venting as a Stress Reduction Tool 90

Outline Your Stress Reduction Plan 92
Conclusion 93

REFERENCES 95

ABOUT THE AUTHOR 101

REVIEW BY DANIEL ECKSTEIN, PH.D. 103

ABOUT THE BOOK 105

INTRODUCTION

Students' conduct in a classroom situation has always been a source of complaints from teachers. The teachers' primary focus is on ensuring that there is effective teaching and learning. Ineffective teaching results occur when students are disruptive and prevent other students' learning.

Included in the number of disruptive behaviour disorders that can cause these disruptions are Oppositional Defiant Disorder (ODD), Conduct Disorder (CD), and Attention Deficit Hyperactive Disorder (ADHD). Symptoms of these disorders present with disruptive behaviour patterns (American Psychiatric Association 2000). In the Jamaican school system, students presenting with these disorders usually face suspension from school. Usually, they are eventually expelled from the school system by age fifteen, because this is the time most behavioural problems seem to exacerbate. The children are usually labelled as rude and lacking in proper home training. Teachers often believe that the presentation of disruptive behaviour is due to low socioeconomic background, since a large number of their students live in poor communities. In my clinical practice, when students who present with a behaviour problem are sent for assessment, teachers typically are hostile; and react to how the student's behaviour is affecting them, rather than to the fact that these children are presenting with a psychological disorder.

The aetiology of the disruptive-behaviour disorders implicates environmental factors. According to Voeller (2004), children who grow up in chaotic environments often have difficulty regulating attention, impulsivity, and emotionality. Research has shown that behaviours seen in children with ADHD are not simply the result of environmental factors or some sort of distortion of perception, but rather are a very real brain dysfunction. In the case of ADHD, studies reveal the dysfunction of the prefrontal subcortical system, often with greater involvement of areas in the right hemisphere (Voeller 2004).

In the United States, about 25 per cent of youths with behaviour and emotional problems are receiving help (Wingenfeld 2002). In comparison, many Jamaican students receive no help because they appear to be rude rather than experiencing psychological problems. However, in response to increasing concerns about students' mental health needs, many schools and school systems have begun to implement approaches to mental health promotion and prevention of mental health problems in school-age children (Wingenfeld 2002).

In response to these concerns, the Jamaican Ministry of Education Youth and Culture (JMOEYC) instituted a groundbreaking programme designed to identify students presenting with behaviour problems so that effective treatment modalities could be put in place to help. The aim of the Program for Alternative Student Support (PASS) is identifying students with disruptive behaviour disorders (JMOEYC 2004). The aim is to plan appropriate treatment so that such students integrate into the mainstream of the school system. Institution of the programme was due to the alarmingly high suspension rate and ultimate expulsion of students presenting with these disorders. This situation has resulted in an increase in violent behaviours in Jamaican society because children expelled from the schools are neither treated nor placed in any rehabilitation programme. Teachers often refuse to work with the children, claiming they are rude, have no proper home training, and that their socioeconomic background predisposes them to these disruptive behaviours.

If teachers understood that these students were presenting with a disorder, the knowledge could greatly aid in alleviating many of the problems caused due to lack of understanding. Teachers' understanding of and involvement in treating disruptive behaviour disorders and ADHD is crucial (Wingenfeld 2002). When teachers do not play an effective role in these children's lives or understand their needs, these students do not perform well within the school system and their behaviour problems worsen. Teachers are the ones who interface with these students on a daily basis and who can play an important role in these children's lives. Because some teachers currently lack knowledge of strategies to deal with students who present with behaviour problems, the current situation in Jamaica is grossly undermining the ability of these students to succeed in the school system.

As mentioned earlier, in Jamaica, a number of these students face suspension from school. The exact percentage of students expelled or suspended from the school system has not been revealed, but the Ministry of Education admits it is significant enough to warrant attention from school authorities. Teachers should be made aware of these disorders in order that they may develop greater understanding. In this way, they will be better able to cope with these students and help them reach their full potential. Understanding disruptive students can help teachers because they will then be able to alert school authorities to ensure that each child presenting with symptoms of disruptive behaviours is assessed, diagnosed, and offered effective treatment.

Psychologists and social workers are now aware of the need to educate teachers about these childhood disorders and which effective strategies to implement. School authorities, too, can also arrange psychoeducational workshops geared towards educating teachers about these disorders so the children's rate of suspension and expulsion from school will decrease. If teachers understood these children, their chances of success in the school system would increase, which would ultimately benefit Jamaican society—dropout and unemployment rates would also decline.

The purpose of this book is to help teachers understand disruptive behaviour disorders and provide useful guides that effectively deal with the students. Psychologists study human behaviour to find ways to solve problems and help people who suffer. We seek that understanding to help both the people with the problem and those who serve them. With that in mind, students presenting with various psychological disorders need understanding of their disorders; and they need their issues addressed in a way that will help them cope with their disorders so that they can live productive lives. Disruptive behaviour disorders present with symptoms that are often debilitating to the children diagnosed with these disorders. A number of individuals are affected when children present with disruptive behaviours including teachers, parents, peers, and society. This solidifies the call that appropriate interventions be put in place to address the issues confronting these students.

I hasten to say this book is by no means exhaustive in addressing the issues relevant to the disruptive behaviour disorders. My intention is to bring into sharp awareness the need for teachers to possess greater understanding of the disruptive disorders. It is then important that an entire book address more in-depth strategies teachers can use to help children presenting with behavioural problems.

CHAPTER 1

Understanding the Disruptive Behaviour Disorders

Bob, age ten, is easily distracted, often fails to give attention to details, and does not appear to listen when spoken to by his teacher. He frequently runs or climbs about, seems to be always on the go, and talks excessively. He blurts out answers and has difficulty waiting his turn.

John, age six, constantly argues with teachers and blatantly refuses to comply with requests made of him. He obeys none of the school rules and takes no blame for the disruptive acts he commits. He uses swear words and foul language. He irritates other children and leaves teachers feeling overwhelmed and frustrated. And in another case, Doug, age 15, displayed cruelty towards animals.

Bob suffers from attention deficit hyperactivity disorder (ADHD), John has oppositional defiant disorder (ODD), and Doug has conduct disorder (CD), all disorders prove challenging to educators because children present with disruptive behaviours that affect both teachers and peers and the teaching/learning process. Bob, John, and Doug are experiencing childhood disruptive behaviour disorders.

The Jamaican school situation indicates that a large number of students present with symptoms of disruptive behaviour disorders

(Pottinger 2001). There is a paucity of research in all areas of study in Jamaican society. Although a review of the literature revealed qualitative studies on issues within Jamaican schools, there is no research specifically related to disruptive behaviour disorders or ADHD.

Pottinger notes that while properly designed studies have not been conducted to identify the rate of ADHD in Jamaica; small samples have shown that about 15–25 per cent of Jamaicans are affected by ADHD (Pottinger 2001). The literature on children with disruptive behaviour disorders shows a remarkable gap between research on childhood psychiatric disorders and teachers' accurate knowledge and implementation of effective strategies. As Lane, Wehby, & Barton-Arwood, (2005) observe, disruptive behaviour tends to become more severe and defiant over time; however, there is ample evidence that current educational practices fail to effectively address the needs of children and youth with disruptive behaviours and ADHD. The consequence of allowing behaviour problems to escalate over time extends beyond the school environment. Children with behaviour problems often become alienated from school and seek escape from school discipline through absenteeism, truancy, and association with antisocial peers (Beebe-Frankenberger, Lane, Bocian, Gresham, & MacMillan 2005).

Children who have concurrent diagnoses of ADHD and CD are at particularly high risk for negative psychosocial outcomes. Individuals with comorbid ADHD and CD exhibit higher degrees of aggression than those with CD alone and are more likely to experience substance abuse problems, and to have problems with the law. Both girls and boys with comorbid ADHD and CD are at high risk for suicidal behaviours; girls, in particular, are prone to drop out of school. Untreated ADHD, ODD, and CD have consequences for the individual and society, but are even more problematic when the disorders coexist. A longitudinal study of clinic-referred and control males found that thirty years later, CD children were more often arrested and imprisoned as adults, were mobile geographically, had more marital difficulties, poorer occupational and economic histories, used alcohol excessively, and to some extent, had poorer physical health (Robin 1974, p.68).

There is no question that teachers experience frustration when faced with disruptive students. However, there is some indication that the way a teacher interacts with a disruptive and ADHD student affects the student's behaviour and the teacher's perception of stress (Greene, Beszterczey, Katzenstein, Park, & Goring 2002). An essential first step for teachers is to possess accurate knowledge of the characteristics of each specific disorder they are likely to encounter in class (Gable 2004; Stevens, Quittner & Abikoff 1998).

ADHD, ODD and CD: Defined

Attention Deficit Hyperactivity Disorder (ADHD)

ADHD is the most common childhood disorder and, consequently, given the most attention in clinical and educational literature. The focus of much of the information in this book is on ADHD (*DSM-IV-TR*, 2000). The criterion for ADHD distinguishes between three basic types of ADHD: predominate inattentive type (ADHD-I); predominately hyperactive-impulsive type (ADHD-H); and combined type (ADHD-C) (APA 2000). Some researchers argue that ADHD follows a developmental pattern beginning with a child's hyperactivity and impulsivity in early childhood, evolving into the combined type during primary school years. The adolescent's symptoms of hyperactivity and impulsiveness diminish as they are faced with increasing demands to act independently in academic and social settings and they become predominately inattentive (Voeller 2004).

Some researchers question the current division between three distinct types of ADHD. However, individuals with ADHD-I typically do not exhibit the disruptive behaviours that characterize ADHD-H and ADHD-C. Children with ADHD-I often remain undiagnosed until they advance into middle school or junior high school grades (Fornarotto & O'Connell 2002). Girls with ADHD are more likely to have ADHD-I, which may contribute to the disproportionate number of boys referred to clinics for exhibiting symptoms of ADHD (Sciutto, Terjesen, & Bender Frank 2004). Clinicians generally agree that ADHD is under diagnosed in girls (Voeller 2004).

ADHD can co-exist with other disorders. The aetiology of ADHD remains poorly understood. Poor parenting, stressful home situations, and neurological defects have all been implicated in the onset of ADHD (Fornarotto & O'Connell 2002). The latest research suggests that a chaotic home life, often associated with ADHD, may also be partly due to a genetic component. More than one-quarter of children with ADHD have parents who meet diagnostic criteria for ADHD (Voeller 2004).

Ideally, ADHD should be managed through team-oriented intervention involving parents, teachers, psychologists, and medical professionals (Fornarotto & O'Connell 2002; Voeller 2004). More globally, educators advocate ongoing collaboration between families, teachers, and service providers for all students with disruptive behaviours (Cheney, Osher, & Caesar 2002). Assessment is also more accurate when data on children's behaviour is collected from a variety of sources and in different social settings (Wingenfeld 2002).

Treatment for ADHD is guided by several key principles (Voeller 2004). The first principle states that the most effective way of managing ADHD is by combining the correct dosage of an appropriate medication with behavioural intervention. An intensive behavioural intervention includes: (a) parent training, (b) individual therapy for the child, (c) school involvement in the behaviour programme and (d) a daily report card completed by the teacher and presented to parents for contingency reinforcement. In conjunction with medication, the behavioural programme has proven more effective than either medication or behavioural treatment alone.

It is important to note another principle for successful treatment of ADHD "involves intensive and prolonged parent involvement and cooperation from the teacher" (Voeller 2004, p. 806). Parent training is an important component, since parents play a key role in helping children develop organized routines, including homework completion and preparation for school each day.

The third principle is that treatment of ADHD should not be confused with treatment of a learning disorder (LD). However, since learning disorders and ADHD frequently overlap, children with ADHD should also be evaluated for LD.

The fourth principle is to ensure that children with ADHD get adequate sleep, nutrition, and exercise. This aspect of managing ADHD is typically overlooked. In fact, many teachers adhere to the belief that curtailing sugar intake will alleviate the symptoms of ADHD, although that assumption has been disproved (Sciutto et al. 2000).

Voeller's (2004) fifth principle is that children with ADHD should be encouraged to develop self-awareness and autonomy. Parents and teachers may undermine children's success by calling them "hyper" or "disorganized" when they display dysfunctional behaviour. Voeller emphasizes that children with ADHD require clear explanations of the problem behaviour and the techniques that will enable them to produce desired outcomes at home and at school. Successful accomplishments should be reinforced and rewarded so that children feel competent and will continue to act appropriately.

This leads to the sixth principle, monitoring the behaviour of children with ADHD and rewarding them when they comply with designated routines. Abiding by this principle is essential to help children complete assignments and hand them in on time.

The seventh principle is of the utmost importance: "Teacher involvement is crucial" (Voeller 2004, p. 808). The problem behaviours that children exhibit in school sometimes emanate from a discrepancy in the behavioural expectations of parents and teachers (Beebe-Frankenberger et al. 2005). For children with ADHD, disparities between home and school expectations can be devastating; ideally, the efforts of parents and teachers should reinforce one another. However, Voeller (2004) also recognizes that there are obstacles to ongoing collaboration between home and school. Highlighting the challenges of managing ADHD, he notes that even when parents and teachers engage in ongoing, intensive communication, changing the behaviour patterns of children with ADHD can take a long time.

Oppositional Defiant Disorder (ODD)

In the United States of America (US), an estimated 2–16 per cent of children are affected by ODD (Fornarotto & O'Connell 2002). Children with ODD typically appear angry and argumentative; they defy rules and authority figures and often they deliberately act to annoy people (APA 2000). At the same time, these children are, themselves, easily annoyed or irritated. They may appear spiteful, vindictive, and resentful, and frequently blame others for their mistakes or transgressions. In fact, a particular challenge for teachers is the inability of children with ODD to take responsibility for their actions (Fornarotto & O'Connell 2002). However, it is important to note that ODD is frequently situational. Although teachers experience problems with children who are defiant in the classroom (Greene et al. 2002), many children display ODD behaviours at home but are compliant in the school setting.

Among younger children, ODD is more common among boys; however, the rates of occurrence in boys and girls converge during adolescence (Fornarotto & O'Connell 2002). ODD is alternately regarded as a precursor to CD and is a milder form of CD. As children mature, the incidence of ODD decreases while the rate of CD increases.

Conduct Disorder (CD)

CD is a severe behavioural disorder characterized by an inability to recognize or respect the basic rights of others and/or the persistent display of socially-defiant behaviour (APA 2000). Children with CD engage in bullying and intimidation of peers, can be cruel to people and animals, and may commit property crimes and violent acts. Repeated school truancy is included in the DSM-IV-TR (2000) diagnostic criteria, as is running away from home overnight or longer. By definition, CD occurs in individuals under the age of eighteen. If the behaviours persist at age eighteen, the individual is classified as having an antisocial personality disorder. Substance abuse problems and trouble with the law are common in children with CD. The prevalence of CD in Jamaica is not known. However, an alarming number of children in Jamaican schools present with behaviours consistent with a diagnosis of CD.

Conduct Disorder has two subtypes: aggressive and nonaggressive (Fornarotto & O'Connell 2002). Children and adolescents with the nonaggressive type engage in actions such as lying, cheating, stealing, and skipping school. Those with the aggressive type commit violent acts such as physical or sexual assault. Children diagnosed with CD prior to age ten are most likely to fall into the aggressive category. Children diagnosed during preadolescence and adolescence were less likely to be aggressive and were more likely to experience positive adjustment as adults.

Oppositional and Defiant Disorder and CD share several risk factors; including low socioeconomic status, inadequate parenting, and having parents with antisocial personality disorder (Fornarotto & O'Connell 2002). Smith & Muenchen (1995), in trying to understand the aetiology of CD, comment that low-income Jamaican families are often characterized by frequent mobility and the absence of a father figure. It is interesting to note that maternal dominance combined with the lack of a father has been linked with irresponsibility, aggression, and low self-esteem among adolescent Jamaican males. In addition, Jamaican parenting practices are frequently very strict, especially for adolescent girls, which may lead girls to become more rebellious and an undermining of their self-worth.

Hickling (1994) observes that a high percentage of Jamaican children with problem behaviour report having aggressive and alcoholic fathers and domineering, manipulative mothers. He disagrees with Smith & Muenchen (1995) that absent fathers contribute to aggressive behaviours in children; and contends that absent fathers seem to be less of a causative factor in the "pathogenesis of illness than the existence of a father/ mother nuclear family with a high level of "interspousal" conflict."

Adolescents with ODD usually perform better in school than adolescents with CD, since they are less likely to be truant or absent, which are actions associated with CD (Fornarotto & O'Connell 2002). However, adolescents with CD are generally more socially adept than those with ODD. The social skills of youth with CD are not necessarily an advantage; therefore, they are likely to seek out the company of antisocial peers, thereby reinforcing defiant norms for behaviour (Beebe-Frankenberger et al. 2005).

Farmer (2000) emphasizes the importance of understanding the social peer dynamics of students who display aggressive and disruptive behaviour in school. Teachers may inadvertently contribute to social structures that encourage defiant, aggressive, or bullying behaviour, either through ineffective disciplinary procedures or through lack of awareness of social hierarchies that exist in class. Farmer contends that effectively targeting intervention entails an understanding of the school context and the social dynamics underlying student behaviour, as well as the individual characteristics of problem students.

Comorbid Behaviour Disorders

Children diagnosed with disruptive behaviour disorders often have another diagnosis running concurrently. When this occurs, the child is presenting with a comorbid diagnosis. Voeller (2004) notes that it is unusual for children to have pure ADHD without a concurrent emotional or learning difficulty (LD). Learning Disorder is the most common condition coexisting with ADHD. Although each condition requires specific intervention in the school setting, even special educators are inadequately prepared to target teaching and support strategies appropriately, according to Gable (2004), who contends that they are likely to possess generic skills for working with disabilities, which they attempt to adapt to students with different disorders.

According to Fornarotto & O'Connell (2002), roughly 35 per cent of individuals with ADHD display behaviours associated with ODD. The prevalent overlap may result in a teacher's failure to recognize students who have ODD without ADHD (Stevens et al. 1998). Working with students who have ADHD comorbid with ODD or CD is far more challenging for teachers than working with students who have ADHD alone. A particular distinction is that children with ADHD are not as likely to intentionally harm or irritate others and are willing to take responsibility for their actions (Fornarotto & O'Connell 2002). This is not the case with children with ODD or CD.

The most serious problem posed by children who have comorbid ADHD and CD is that they display more severe manifestations of ADHD as well as higher aggression than individuals with only ADHD or with ADHD and ODD. Ultimately, these children are at the highest risk for negative consequences, including incarceration as juveniles or adults.

Teachers' Perceptions and Knowledge of Disruptive Behaviour Disorders

Teachers value certain behaviours in their students, behaviours they deem important to effective classroom functioning. In order to understand teachers' attitudes towards students who present with disruptive behaviour, it is important to examine classroom behaviours deemed important for academic and social success. Lane, Pierson, & Givner (2003, p.426) state that "students whose social and behavioural repertoires are aligned with teachers' expectations are more likely to experience desirable outcomes with both peers and adults;" whereas, those whose behaviour runs counter to teachers' perceptions of good behaviour are at risk for negative outcomes beyond the school environment. Teachers, therefore, do not want to confront certain problems in the classroom.

According to Poulou & Norwich (2000), the major problems teachers do not want to confront in the classroom include: work avoidance, a depressive mood, negativism, school phobia, offensive language, disobedience, difficulties in cooperation, lack of concentration, truancy, physical aggression, hindering other children, and withdrawal from common activities. These behaviours are defining characteristics of ADHD, ODD, and CD. In the Poulou & Norwich study, the teachers reported spending the greatest amount of class time dealing with these students, as well as spending additional time reflecting on appropriate management strategies. They identified lack of concentration as the most prevalent problem behaviour, and one of the most challenging, underscoring one of the problems presented by ADHD. Other behaviours highlighted by the teachers were talking without permission, untidiness, and fidgeting. These behaviours were viewed as annoying rather than disruptive (Poulou & Norwich 2000).

Teachers' education programmes invariably fail to prepare student teachers for the realities of classroom management. Kokkinos, Panayiotou, & Davazoglou (2004), note that the term "reality shock" has been used to describe the experience of teacher interns confronting the issue of classroom management for the first time. Inadequate preparation is especially detrimental for teachers of students with disruptive behaviour disorders and ADHD. Teachers may inadvertently trigger disruptive behaviour through teaching strategies or classroom practices that frustrate students (Gable 2004). Gable notes that teachers who fail to accommodate students with special needs may unwittingly sabotage their efforts to establish classroom discipline.

Teachers were asked to identify the most serious disruptive behaviours displayed by students. Teachers targeted antisocial behaviours such as stealing, cruelty and bullying, and vandalizing school property (Kokkinos et al. 2004). These behaviours coincide with diagnostic criteria for CD (DSM-IV-TR 2000). If teachers are not equipped to understand these behaviours, it is no wonder that teacher trainees experience culture shock when confronted with students displaying disruptive behaviours.

Teachers' Experiences With and Attitudes towards ADHD, ODD, and CD Students

Teachers have certain expectations regarding what constitutes appropriate classroom behaviour. Students with disruptive behaviour very often do not display the teachers' desired behaviours. There are ample indications that students with disruptive behaviours are especially stressful to teach. At the same time, teachers found it significantly more stressful to teach children with ADHD who exhibited oppositional/aggressive behaviour than to teach children with ADHD who did not exhibit concurrent behaviour problems.

Interacting with students with ADHD consumed a substantial amount of the teachers' time. Although the teachers engaged in significantly more negative interactions with students with ADHD, Greene et al. (2002) emphasize that teachers also engaged in positive and neutral interactions with these students and propose that the individual variations in stress experienced by teachers working with students with ADHD may be due to the quality of the teacher-student relationships. Teachers who find students less stressful may provide more positive support which, in turn, encourages more appropriate classroom behaviours.

According to Albert (1989), mistakes teachers make when dealing with disruptive students are:

(a) getting mad and responding accordingly;

(b) reacting publicly;

(c) taking the position that it's not their concern, that someone else should deal with it;

(d) referring the student to the principal or guidance counsellors for straightening out;

(e) raising their voice;

(f) yelling; and

(g) using tense body language, such as a rigid posture, or clenched fists.

Teachers persist in using these strategies although they are not effective.

Despite the importance of the school in ensuring proper behaviour of students, relatively few teachers have sufficient knowledge about the foundations and principles of treatment concerning ADHD, nor do they receive adequate training to deal with ADHD-related problems in the classroom (Frolich, Dopfner, Biegert, & Lehmkuhl 2002). Bekle (2004) carried out a study to compare practicing teachers' knowledge and undergraduate education students' knowledge and attitudes about ADHD and found there were some knowledge gaps; although, both practicing teachers and undergraduate students possessed sound information about ADHD. Teachers expressed a desire for comprehensive training. The results of this study show some discrepancy with similar research conducted by Jerome, Gordon, & Hustler (1994), who found that teachers' knowledge of the disorders is too inadequate to be effective in controlling classroom disruptive behaviours. The latter study concurs with a study conducted by the author with Jamaican teachers that showed their knowledge of the disorder was inadequate, thus affecting their effectiveness in dealing with disruptive students. The implications of the findings suggest the need for development in academia and in-service teacher training.

Teachers' Reactions and Intervention Strategies

Teachers value certain student behaviours that will ensure effective classroom management. Since ADHD, ODD, or CD students display behaviours that are not congruent with effective classroom functioning, teachers compound the problem because they lack knowledge and appropriate methods of intervention that could help disruptive students reach their potential. In a study of secondary high schools in Jamaica, Evans (2001) investigated teachers' reactions to students who misbehaved and asserted that when students challenge teachers' authority and experience problems in learning, teachers' responses ranged from resignation and frustration to disdain, contempt, and hostility. Some teachers adopted an approach that combined punishment and coercion with disrespect. Evans concluded that teachers had low expectations for these students and were not prepared to find out or address their learning needs.

Reis, E.M. (2002) implicates teachers' lack of awareness of the negative classroom environments they create. In working with three classroom teachers whose classes contained students with ADHD, Reis notes that teachers often berated these students for lack of focused attention, for talking out of turn, or for engaging in distracting behaviours. However, once the teachers were made aware of the frequency with which they did this and were presented with positive comments they could use to reward effort and enhance motivation, they made the appropriate changes. The teachers' use of positive comments was reinforced by results. Reis, (2002, p.176) notes "The teachers were truly amazed at the effort the students demonstrated in response to the positive comments as well as the decrease in the frequency in which negative behaviours occurred".

Teachers generally respond negatively to disruptive behaviour and disordered children. A number of behaviour modification programmes have been implemented in the United States to help children with disruptive behaviours to reach their potential despite having a behavioural disorder. The Jamaican school system has taken some steps towards addressing the problem, but we can safely say it is a work in progress.

Evans (2001) carried out an ethnographic study to investigate why students misbehaved and were disruptive in class. Evans also sought to ascertain how teachers responded to students when they were being disruptive. Findings revealed that teachers sometimes punished students by refusing to award them grades for work done. The entire class could be punished by being given a nil grade because of the behaviour of one child. When teachers were admonishing, informing, or correcting, the tone was often hostile, uncaring, sarcastic, or disrespectful. The research carried out by Evans (2001) addressed behaviour problems in classrooms in Jamaica. Nonetheless, many of the behavioural problems identified in her research are consistent with characteristics displayed by ADHD, ODD, and CD students. This underscores the point that teachers' reaction and intervention strategies are usually reactive rather than proactive without well-defined behaviour modification strategies.

Several experts contend that the first step in managing problem behaviours in class is self-reflection on the part of the teacher (Palardy & Palardy 1987; Richardson & Shupe 2003). A crucial factor in the success of classroom interventions is the teacher's belief that students are capable of acting appropriately (Palardy & Palardy 1987). Teachers convey positive expectations by involving students in setting up classroom rules, by clearly publishing rules for behaviour, and above all, by rewarding good behaviour. Although there is some controversy about the use of extrinsic rewards in class (critics argue that this diminishes intrinsic motivation), there is unanimous support for the use of praise and positive feedback (Witzel & Mercer 2003). Verbal awards enhance academic and social motivation for students with disruptive behaviour disorders.

One thing that teachers are typically unaware of is that their own behaviour can trigger outbursts from students with disruptive behaviour disorders (Richardson & Shupe 2003). Much of the power of reframing is due to its ability to defuse potential conflict (Tyler & Jones 2002; Weiner 2003). According to Richardson & Shupe (2003), teachers who are cognizant of their own emotional processes are more likely to reduce classroom conflicts such as power struggles with students.

In addition to understanding the way their behaviour affects students, teachers must be aware of the various contexts in which problem behaviours occur: at the beginning of class, at the end of the class, or as the weekend approaches. Palardy and Palardy (1987, p.89) notes that, "Knowing when students will present with problem behaviours is an important first step in planning to prevent them". In essence, adopting a proactive approach is the best strategy for averting problem behaviour or defusing the situation when problem behaviour occurs.

Emphasizing the vital importance of creating a positive learning environment, Jenson, Olympia, Farley, and Clark (2004, p.72) state that, "Self-management strategies are some of the most effective approaches for students with externalizing disorders to influence the 'positiveness' of their academic environment". Elements of self-management programmes include self-monitoring and self-evaluation, as well as techniques designed to elicit positive feedback and praise from teachers. Self-management strategies help students gain a sense of self-efficacy by allowing them to feel in control of their behaviour and its outcomes. Teachers find self-management strategies effective for increasing engagement and decreasing disruptive behaviour in students with ADHD (Reis 2002).

Conclusion

Despite an accumulating body of research on behaviour disorders, particularly ADHD, teachers have limited knowledge of the needs of students with disruptive behaviour disorders or of classroom management and instructional strategies for working with them successfully. Experts are unanimous in supporting the use of praise and positive reinforcement as a powerful tool for reducing problem behaviour and improving academic performance. However, there is extensive evidence that teachers' reactions to students with ADHD, ODD, and CD are generally negative, which can trigger disruptive behaviour and further exacerbate behaviour-disordered students' problems. Most teachers lack in-service and pre-service training in the behaviour disorders and are largely unaware of the various behaviour management strategies they can apply in the classroom, including self-management techniques which can be very effective.

Among students with ADHD, peer rejection and academic difficulties are the most prevalent problems. Ideally, ADHD can be managed via a comprehensive approach that includes medication, behavioural intervention, and parental involvement. ODD is often a precursor to CD, the most severe behaviour disorder. Students with concurrent CD and ADHD represent a particular challenge to teachers and are at higher risk for negative consequences beyond the school environment. The literature indicates that positive, school-based strategies such as assertive discipline and an ecosystem approach can successfully reach students with serious, persistent behaviour problems. Successfully implementing these programmes requires specialized training and collaborative support that is typically lacking in most schools.

CHAPTER 2

Jamaican Teachers' Experiences With and Attitudes towards ADHD, ODD and CD Students

In a recent study I conducted in 2006, Jamaican teachers' experiences with disruptive students revealed a number of findings. Twenty teachers, consisting of 2 males and 18 females, were interviewed. Their teaching experience ranged from 18 months to 45 years. Regarding teachers, 20 per cent had experience ranging from 0–5 years; 5 per cent had between 6–10 years of experience; 15 per cent had 16–20 years of experience; and 5 per cent had between 21–25 years of experience. Thirty per cent had over 25 years in teaching. All participants in the study were teaching boys with the disorders in question, but they had taught girls in the past. The teachers ranged in age from 22–60 years old. In regard to the challenges faced by the teachers, 35 per cent of them were teaching students with ADHD; 15 per cent with ADHD and CD; 20 per cent with ADHD,CD and ODD; 10 per cent with ODD and CD; 15 per cent with CD; and 5 per cent of the interviewees were teaching students with only ODD.

Teachers' qualifications included certificates, diplomas, bachelor's degrees, and master's degrees. A diploma in teaching is awarded by

Jamaican teachers' colleges. Advanced degrees usually are awarded by universities in the United States of America and the University of the West Indies (UWI). Twelve teachers, 60 per cent of those in my study, had diplomas in teaching, whereas only one had a certificate, the lowest form of teacher qualification in the Jamaican education system. A combination of teacher's diploma and BA degrees were held by 35 per cent of the teachers, and one teacher held a Master of Arts degree in educational administration. The teachers who participated in the study were highly qualified as evidenced by their certification of first degrees and master's degrees. Most of the teachers held diplomas in teaching with advanced degrees in guidance and counselling, and in educational administration.

When teachers were asked what the disorders under review were, all the teachers described both the characteristics of the disorder and the child's disruptive behaviour patterns. Nineteen teachers, including teachers with advanced degrees, could not adequately say what the disorders were or how to effectively deal with students presenting with these disorders. Nineteen teachers reported that teacher training colleges did not prepare them to teach disruptive students. When teachers were asked, "What is your experience teaching a disruptive student?" they described a variety of disruptive behaviour patterns displayed by the ADHD children. All of the teachers described out-of-seat activities, such as children wanting to sharpen a pencil, or asking to leave the class when being seated was required, or interfering with other students by hitting, pinching, or taking away other students' things. Students would blurt out answers and often did not complete classroom work or homework.

All of the teachers described characteristics of the disorders and described the children's disruptive behaviour patterns. Teachers' experiences with these students were generally negative. They were frustrated, angry, annoyed, and described their interactions with these students as difficult, hard, challenging, and at times irritating. "Frustration" was the word used by nineteen teachers to describe their feelings about ODD and CD or ADHD. Teachers' responses to the question about their feelings towards ODD and CD elicited a more intense emotion of anger, and they used words such as "irritating" and "annoying" to describe their feelings about the ADHD child. Two of the twenty teachers described their feelings as "stressed". The teachers also gave a number of reasons why they were frustrated:

(a) A lack of knowledge about the disorder;

(b) A lack of resources both from the school and from the Ministry of Education;

(c) The students' consistently disruptive behaviour;

(d) Parental non-support;

(e) A lack of strategy to deal with these students;

(f) Large class sizes that made it difficult to deal with disruptive behaviour; and

(g) The fact that college did not prepare them to deal with disruptive and ADHD students.

Teachers described a variety of behaviour patterns that led to disruption of the teaching/learning process. For example, (a) students displayed inattention and impulsivity, which affected their ability to stay focused; (b) students' behaviour was manifested by interrupting other students and by irritating or causing bodily harm to other students (in the case of ADHD); and (c) students frequently defied the teacher's attempt to control or focus them.

Teachers reported that they responded to disruptive behaviour-disordered students in a number of ways. They would shout, yell, send the child out of the class, use children to run errands, beat or slap, look at the child angrily, suspend, or ignore. Teachers also described positive reactions, but this was dependent on whether the child was displaying appropriate classroom behaviours. All of the teachers commented that the Ministry of Education was not doing enough to help them cope with disruptive students. Teachers were asked how they saw other teachers reacting to disruptive behaviour-disordered children. All described their reactions as less intense than those of other teachers and believed that they were not equipped to deal with the students. They recommended that each school should have special educators. Two of the twenty teachers believed that ODD and CD students should be placed in special classes and should not be in the regular school system. They believed that they should be given counselling to help the students modify their inappropriate behaviour.

Teachers reported that ODD and CD students were suspended, had their parents called in, and were sent out of the class more often than ADHD students. Two of the twenty teachers described their reaction in terms of strategies they use to help modify students' behaviour. Teachers listed yelling as one of the reactions to disruptive students. The results of the research indicated that:

1. Teachers' responses were characterized by an absence of any coordinated plans or strategies based on research or knowledge about the problem. Teachers' general reaction to disruptive students was to shout/yell, give a cold stare, give timeout, send the student to the guidance office, call in parents, use corporal punishment, and ignore or abandon students. Teachers mainly used ad hoc methods to try to control students' behaviour.

2. Teachers had more intense reactions towards ODD and CD students than towards students with ADHD.

3. Teachers displayed positive attitudes towards students when students displayed appropriate behaviours.

4. Teachers who developed negative reactions to students frequently manifested negative views towards other teachers who did the same thing.

Teachers had different attitudes towards girls who present with disruptive behaviours than boys.

1. Teachers described different behaviour patterns displayed by boys and girls. Girls displayed more internalizing behaviours but were also inclined to create division in the class. Boys displayed more externalizing behaviours and were more disruptive than girls.

2. Teachers did not expect disruptive behaviours from girls but expected boys to be disruptive.

3. Teachers believed they did not treat boys differently from girls; but even though they were aware of gender stereotypes, they often treated the sexes differently.

According to Lane et al. (2003), teachers value certain behaviours in students and the behaviour of the disruptive child is not consistent with the desired classroom behaviours. Teachers want to ensure effective teaching and learning. Because these students' behaviours are not congruent with the teachers' expectations, the teachers develop negative attitudes towards these students. This appears to be because teachers lack general knowledge and understanding of the disorder. Teachers' discussions concerning classroom behaviour is certainly not a new subject. As early as the 1920s, in a landmark study, Wickman (1928) showed that teachers ranked misbehaviour in the classroom as a serious problem (Green et al. 2002). If teachers rank misbehaviour as serious, and lack knowledge as to the cause for these behaviours that are classified as disruptive, then they will view these students in a negative way.

Since Wickman's study, an extensive body of knowledge has developed concerning disruptive behaviour disorders. One conclusion that can be drawn from my study is that the teachers have not made adequate use of the knowledge base of the disruptive disorders. The teachers erroneously believe that the students can control their behaviours and that the student is being disruptive because of his or her parents' inability to provide proper home training. The aetiology of the disruptive disorders is poorly understood. Poor parenting, stressful home situations, and neurological defects have all been implicated in the onset of ADHD (Fornarotto & O'Connell 2002), but the teachers believe that poor parenting is the sole cause of disruptive behaviours. This has led them to label students as rude, thus contributing to the general negative attitudes displayed by the teachers in this study. If teachers label these students negatively, their negative and disruptive behaviours will only be reinforced. The implication of research findings is that poor, non-supportive teaching places disruptive students at risk for poor performance and exacerbates their disruptive behaviour patterns.

Knowledge about the causes of these disorders helps teachers towards a better understanding of how to cope with these students. Moreover, the implications are that if disruptive children display behaviours that are inappropriate for effective classroom functioning and if teachers are unaware of the causes of the disorder, then they will not know how to effectively deal with these students. It was evident from my research that teachers lacked the expertise to deal with disruptive students. The research of Sciutto et al. (2000) supports the finding that teachers' knowledge of the disorders was limited. He concluded that teachers' knowledge of ADHD was restricted to symptoms. Vereb & DiPerna (2004) support the findings of Sciutto et al. (2000). They stressed the need for teachers to get accurate information on treatment modalities, particularly on behavioural strategies that they can implement in the classroom. A similar conclusion was drawn from my research. Teachers need both pre-service and in-service training in the behaviour disorders in order to put strategies into effect that will help to modify these students' behaviour.

According to Semmler (2001), teachers need to research the disability and provide the best solution possible. The teachers in my study evidently had done no research on the disorders. Teachers often were unable to find appropriate solutions that could help to maximize disruptive students' learning potential. Teachers reported that they were not educated about behaviour disorders during their teacher training courses. They were given basic classroom management techniques, but not knowledge of disruptive disorders. If teachers genuinely believed that students were suffering from a psychological disorder and not just being rude because of poor home training, they would implement classroom management strategies geared to help manage problem behaviours.

Based on the findings of the study, a number of questions need answers. Do teachers see caring for disruptive students as part of their responsibility? Are teacher trainers aware of the prevalence of disruptive disorders? Why is pre-service training not given? If teachers feel they are not responsible enough to educate themselves about the disorders, who are the ones responsible? It becomes very evident that since pre-service training is not given, then there is a need for in-service training of teachers. The implications are evident that there is need for greater awareness of these disorders and in-service training provided for teachers.

According to Semmler (2001), in the United States of America 3–5 per cent of children have ADHD. In Jamaican society, it appears to be more widespread. This means that a large number of children present with symptoms of disruptive behaviours. The implication of such a finding is evident. A teacher is bound to encounter a student suffering from this disorder at some time in his/her career. This means that every teacher should be prepared. Teachers in the study were ill-prepared and ill-equipped to deal with these students.

Stevens et al. (1998) recommend that teachers be educated on all childhood disorders so that teachers will be able to recognize the unique symptomatology of each disorder. Sciutto et al. (2000) agree that teachers require accurate knowledge of childhood disorders. My research findings support that of Sciutto et al. (2000). Teachers were trying to modify students' behaviour but lacked the prerequisite knowledge. This lack of knowledge resulted in unfocused strategies that served to exacerbate students' disruptive behaviours. Knowledge of disruptive disorders may help teachers in designing behaviour modification programmes to ensure appropriate behaviours so that students maximize their learning potential.

Teachers in my study appear to be left on their own to cope with disruptive students. The implication of such a situation is clear; teachers are not only faced with disruptive students, but do not have the necessary support system in place to make dealing with these students less stressful. They appear to be ignorant of the disorders or are unwilling to find solutions for themselves. Teachers in the Jamaican school system are usually underpaid and they must contend with disruptive students without adequate resources. This could lead them to develop negative attitudes, thus further undermining their effectiveness in helping these students. If teachers feel unsupported, it makes sense that they will feel stress.

Many of the teachers I interviewed had to contend with large classes, and many of the classes were open pod. A number of teachers had a student-teacher ratio of 45:1 and had to contend with disruptive students. These large class sizes make it difficult to manage a disruptive child. Weiner (2003) observes that large class size makes classroom management challenging. Studies done in the United States have yielded similar results. The research of Lane et al. (2003) suggests that the large class size typical of US high schools makes it difficult for teachers to manage disruptive students in mainstream classes. These findings support teachers' complaints of feeling that their problems with disruptive students are compounded when they teach large class sizes containing disruptive students. This situation would lead to teachers feeling frustrated because their goals and objectives are not met.

Research has shown that people who feel angry, powerless, and out of control, often feel powerless because they do not understand what they are facing. This is because they feel ill-prepared and ill-equipped. They tend to get angry and frustrated because they do not know how to carry out their plans to satisfy their goals. Teachers that I interviewed admitted to not knowing about the disorders and to being ill-equipped to deal with these students. If teachers are ill-equipped and ill-prepared, this could lead to the frustration and anger they describe when interfacing with disruptive students.

Teachers' problems with disruptive students were also compounded because of non—support from parents. Although the issue of parental support was not a question asked by the researcher in the initial interviews, it became a recurring answer to the question of why teachers were frustrated. Teachers said their frustration arose because they often did not get any support from parents. Parents seldom came to school to inquire about their children; they would accompany their children to school on the day of registration and would not be seen again. Parents did not support homework or school activities that require parental involvement. According to Fornarotto and O'Connell (2002) and Voeller (2004), management of ADHD should be through team-oriented intervention involving parents, teachers, psychologists, and medical professionals. The same holds true for CD and ODD.

Farmer (2000) underscores the importance of understanding disruptive students. Teachers may inadvertently contribute to and exacerbate disruptive behaviours in their classes. All the teachers in the study reacted to disruptive behaviours in different ways, depending largely on how disruptive the behaviour was and on the frequency of the behaviour on any given day. Teachers would shout or yell, send the student out of the class, use children to run errands, flog, ignore the child when he was misbehaving, give a cold stare, or abandon the child. Students in high school were suspended; parents were called in and students frequently were sent to the principal's office and the guidance counsellor's office.

Shouting and yelling exacerbate disruptive students' behaviour problems, according to Albert (1989). The teachers' reactions observed from my research serve only to heighten the degree of the disruptive child's behaviour. The teachers' general reactions towards these students were that these students either should be in special classes in the schools, with special educators, or placed in special schools that would cater to their special needs. All the teachers believed that schools should have special educators to help these students, because they were not equipped to deal with disruptive students

Classic mistakes teachers make when dealing with disruptive students is in how they react negatively to students; thus, not achieving their desired results to get students behaving appropriately. According to Albert (1989), mistakes teachers make when dealing with disruptive students are (a) getting mad and responding accordingly; (b) reacting publicly; (c) taking the position that it is not their concern, that someone else should deal with it; (d) referring the student to the principal or guidance counsellors for straightening out; (e) raising their voice; (f) yelling; and (g) using tense body language, such as a rigid posture, or clenched fists. Teachers who participated in my study used all of these techniques. Teachers recognize that these techniques do not work, yet they persisted in using them; hence, the frustration they experience.

The literature indicates that parents and teachers may undermine children's success by calling them "hyper" or "disorganized" when they display dysfunctional behaviour. The teachers I observed undermined disruptive students' success by the way they reacted to them. Teachers commented that these students often do not succeed in the school system and that they eventually end up not accomplishing much in society. Teachers who generally react in negative ways to students lack the strategies needed to promote effective classroom management.

It could be concluded, based on teachers' responses, that they, too, form part of the disruptive students' problem. Voeller (2004) emphasizes that children with ADHD require clear explanations of the problem behaviour and of the techniques that will enable them to produce the desired outcomes at home and at school.

Teachers in the research displayed positive reactions towards students with disruptive behaviours, but this was contingent on desired behaviour from the child. Some of the same teachers who display negative attitudes towards these students also display positive reactions, depending largely on appropriate behaviours being displayed by the disruptive students. Some teachers developed strategies to help modify students' behaviour.

Admittedly, disruptive behaviour disordered children are challenging to teach, and teachers need to employ effective classroom management techniques. One teaching behaviour that is widely recognized as an effective practice is to provide praise for both correct academic responses and appropriate social behaviour.

A number of teachers in the study employed praise when students displayed desired behaviours. However, the greater number of teachers had no strategies. Sutherland (2000) observes that effective instructional practices with sound empirical support are not often observed in classrooms where there are students with behaviour disorders. The literature on children with behaviour disorders indicates that effective strategies must be employed to modify the students' behaviour. A comprehensive treatment program should include a combination of medication and behavioural intervention. Included in the behavioural program is a system of positive reinforcement. The teachers I interviewed did not have structured effective behavioural modification programs to help these students.

Teachers who developed negative reactions towards students, frequently manifested negative views towards other teachers who did the same thing. Research has shown that powerless, angry, frustrated people who do not know what to do sometimes resort to aggression (Feldman 2001). One of the most influential and durable explanations for human aggression, states that frustration and aggression are closely linked (Feldman 2001). The teachers in this study are frustrated with themselves, the school system; and therefore, they feel powerless. This powerlessness leads them to displacing their frustration on other teachers.

Teachers I interviewed were angry, frustrated, and felt helpless. A number of teachers in my research resorted to punishing, yelling, and flogging students. When feelings of helplessness persist, teachers experience cognitive dissonance. They think to themselves, "I am a teacher; I am supposed to ensure that students learn, but I spend most of my teaching time spanking, yelling, and sending students out of the classroom". The dissonance experienced by some teachers leads them to develop guilt and anxiety. They then resort to the defence mechanism of projection. Often people who experience guilt project it onto their associates. A logical conclusion is that the teachers are not aware that their reactions are just as negative as that of the teacher they are criticizing. One implication is that their reactions will lead to morale problems in the schools. It could affect the esprit de corps of the teaching staff in the affected schools, ultimately leading to staff division and competition. All the teachers in my study displayed negative attitudes towards disruptive behaviour disorder students, yet many believed they had positive attitudes towards these students. This finding supports the study done by Jenson et al. (2004), who note that teachers' self-perceptions of being positive do not necessarily correspond to classroom observation. Teachers tended to overestimate their use of positive strategies.

Teachers' general reaction to ADHD was to shout or yell, to give a cold stare, or to put a child in timeout. All teachers agreed that these students need special educators, but teachers also said the ODD and CD students need counselling and should not be a part of the regular class because of the danger they pose to other children. Teachers normally react to these students in a number of ways: (a) using timeouts under watchful supervision; (b) sending the student to the guidance counsellor's or principal's office; (c) calling in the student's parents; or (d) ignoring the behaviour, and taking the attitude that if the child wants to learn, learning will occur, but that there is nothing the teacher can do with this child. Only one of the twenty teachers believed that these students should be given medication as a treatment modality.

Teachers see these students not only as disruptive but also as a threat to teachers and students. The teachers see ODD and CD students as dangerous, as they invoke fear in their peers. ODD and CD children at the junior high level are not expelled from the school. The teachers' attitude is that these students will continue to drift through the system with a series of punishments and suspensions. However, these measures do not work because once the children return to school, there is a recurrence of the behaviour pattern. Teachers become frustrated because they cannot help, so the problem persists.

The teachers' differences in attitude towards ODD and CD students according to Fornarotto and O'Connell (2002), indicate a particular distinction due to the fact that children with ADHD do not intentionally harm or irritate others and are willing to take responsibility for their actions. ODD—or CD-affected children, on the other hand, tend to harm others. Children with ODD exhibit high levels of hostility towards peers. Defiant and oppositional behaviours can lead to conflict with teachers, their peers, their parents, and their siblings.

The teachers I observed tended to have a different feeling towards ADHD children. Teachers viewed ADHD children as frustrating, just as they did the ODD and CD students, but they used softer words to describe their experiences with the ADHD students, such as "annoying", "irritating", and "challenging". Teachers wanted to help these students; however, they also believed that they were not equipped to deal with these students in the regular school system. They believe it is virtually impossible to help these children when they have to teach classes with a student-teacher ratio of 45:1. Teachers tended to use more focused strategies with ADHD than with ODD and CD students. Teachers gave ADHD children more timeouts, gave rewards for good behaviour, called in their parents less, and seldom sent ADHD students to the principal's office, compared to the ODD and CD students.

Teachers generally had negative attitudes towards all disruptive students, but they displayed more intense negative attitudes towards ODD and CD students. A review of the literature reveals that students with ODD and CD are more prone to display behaviours that lead to conflict with teachers (Harada et al. 2002). The implications are that both sets of students are at risk of not reaching their academic potential, because teachers lack understanding of the disorders. However, the ODD and CD students are more likely to face hostility from teachers, are more likely to face suspension, and drift through the school system without proper intervention. Because of this, they are apt to move into society untreated with the likelihood that their disorder will transition into antisocial personality disorder.

Disruptive behaviours tend to become more severe and recalcitrant over time, yet there is ample evidence that current educational practices fail to effectively address the needs of children and youths with disruptive behaviours and ADHD (Lane 2005). Children who have concurrent diagnoses of ADHD and CD are at particularly high risk of negative psychological outcomes (Fornarotto & O'Connell 2002). ADHD students, because they find it difficult to be attentive for sustained periods, fail to make the most of class time. Teachers have few strategies to deal with them, so these students face the risk of not reaching their full academic potential. Therefore, it can be concluded that these disorders, if they go untreated and are not understood by teachers, could have implications for the children and for Jamaican society, which is currently plagued by crime and violence. Further research should be made regarding whether there is a correlation between violence in the Jamaican society and children with disruptive behaviour disorders.

This observation is in keeping with findings from Beebe-Frankenberger et al. (2005), who demonstrated the consequences of allowing behaviour problems to escalate over grades and extending beyond the school environment. Children with behaviour problems often become alienated from school and seek escape from school discipline through absenteeism, truancy, and association with antisocial peers. If ADHD, ODD, and CD go untreated, it could have grave implications for society. The current findings serve to bring to the attention of school personnel the current state of affairs regarding how teachers interface with disruptive students. It should also alert psychologists and social workers to the need to carry out effective assessments and to provide support for teachers. My research suggests that teachers' attitudes towards these students are undermining their success in school and feedback on this issue would be helpful to teachers. Further research to support this finding would be useful. The study suggests that knowledge of the disorders could result in the reduction of teachers' stress levels. School could also provide stress management workshops to help them cope. It also suggests that the dissonance faced by teachers when confronted with these students could be significantly reduced if teachers gained greater understanding of these disorders.

The teachers described the disruptive behaviour patterns of the sexes. Among younger children, ODD is more common in boys. The majority of the schools that participated in the study were primary and junior high schools and this could account for the prevalence of boys with the disorder. Boys display more externalizing behaviour patterns, whereas girls do more internalizing. The behaviour that ODD and CD girls display is alarming to teachers because they do not expect girls to behave in such a manner.

A review of the literature indicates that gender bias is prevalent among teachers. According to Pisecco et al. (2001) and Sciutto et al. (2004), there is some indication of gender bias in the way teachers interact with boys and girls. According to Evans (2001), in interviews with students, both males and females acknowledged that teachers treated boys and girls differently. Both boys and girls admitted that boys received more harsh and unfair treatment than girls did. Evans's study found that boys are more likely to receive corporal punishment and insults from teachers. In the study, 18 per cent of boys, compared with 10 per cent of girls, reported receiving corporal punishment in school. The study concluded that both boys and girls experienced negative practices and treatment at school, but that boys were likely to experience more negative interactions than girls were.

Jamaican Teachers' Qualitative Responses about Disruptive Disorders

When teachers were asked about their experience teaching ADHD, the teachers described the symptomologies of the disorders. These are excerpts from the teachers' responses. Ms O. described the characteristics of the ADHD child in her class:

"The child would always be hitting, pinching, or interfering with others. He darts out of the class. It is difficult for him to stay still. He would not sit at a table with other children. He would blurt out answers but often had the incorrect answers. He would not complete tasks."

Ms C. teaches at the primary and the junior high levels of education. She has been in teaching for the past twenty years. She teaches an eight-year-old boy with ADHD and believes that 75 per cent of her class display behaviour characteristics of ADHD. She states, "Well, as a matter of fact, 75 per cent of my class is ADHD because I have the lower stream." Ms C., like the other teachers, related her experience by talking about the characteristics of ADHD:

"He does not sit still, you talk to him this moment and while you are talking to him he is doing something else, such as picking on other students."

Ms F. has been teaching for over nine years. She teaches the ten—and eleven-year-olds in a primary and junior high school. She teaches two students, one with ADHD and the other with ODD or CD. She was very animated in her responses and at times dramatized the actions the students displayed in her class. Ms F. gave the following response to the question of her experience teaching these students, It centred on the students' behaviour patterns:

"I have this particular boy, who, when given certain exercises to do, he will say, 'Teacher, I cannot do those things'. He may sit down and begin to write in his book and by the time you look around, he is not there. He comes in again to find someone to play with, and then he is out of the class again. He is always disturbing other teachers' class."

She described how the ADHD boy disturbs her class:

"He disturbs his other classmates. He walks around with a piece of stick and knocks the desk, then he goes outside again, provokes the children—basically, that kind of behaviour."

Ms S. has been teaching for the past twenty-nine years. She presents herself as a very no-nonsense person. She has gone on to further studies and has a BSc. degree. She currently teaches a ten-year-old boy with ADHD. She related her experience teaching this student:

"When you are ready to start your class, this is when this child wants to sharpen a pencil, buy a book, and drink water. This is the time he will not give you the attention. He will be reading another book that we are not currently using. He gets up out of his seat when being seated is what is required. He will not pay attention. This could disrupt the class and valuable teaching time is lost. At the end of the session, the students have not grasped anything. At the end of the session, you will do your evaluation and discover that these children have learned nothing, because they respond inappropriately. This boy succeeds in keeping back those students who should be doing better. The long and short of it is, at the end of the school year when it is time to measure what students have done with various tests of performance, it is thrown back at you that your own performance standard is below grade level and you are not working. When students have these problems, they are not singled out and given specific help. How, then, do you expect them to perform and perform well?"

Ms T. is a grade two teacher and has been teaching for twenty-five years. She teaches eight-year-olds and teaches an eight-year-old boy with ADHD. She stated:

> "You ask the students to sit and some of the time to take part in what you are doing. Sometimes they try to distract other students, showing them something or doing some form of activities that will draw attention to them . . .
>
> "The child cannot find his pencil, or his books. He starts to walk around other children who are trying to do their work. He interrupts the children, although he knows it is not his books. I would direct him to his seat; he would sit for a while and start the process of walking around the class all over . . . He rarely produces work and oftentimes no work at all. He rarely does his homework. He likes to speak out of turn."

Ms G. teaches at a primary and junior high school and has been in teaching for the past thirty-two years. One cannot tell that she has been teaching for such a long period because she speaks with such energy and enthusiasm about teaching. Ms G. thinks that there is a general lack of discipline now prevalent in the schools. She related her experience teaching a ten-year-old ADHD boy. She responded to the statement, "Tell me your experience teaching this boy" in the following manner:

> Ms G.: "It is good, interesting too, but I must tell you, you need God's assistance, patience; you need to be strong, learn to give love and be careful."
>
> Interviewer: "Be careful?"

Ms G: "Yes, very careful, because the way these children are, you want to apply different punishment, including slapping them, so you have to be careful."

Ms G. commented further on her experience teaching a behaviour disordered student:

"He cannot sit still. I asked the child to sit, he moves about the classroom. I grab him by the hand and tell him to sit. He sits for a while, and then he is up again. He interrupts other children. When work is given, he will write two words and then get up again. He does not complete work . . .

"I teach a very large class. It takes a while before the class is settled so that I can start teaching. This boy's behaviour leads to fights in the class. Other children in the class want to learn, but this child constantly disrupts the class. As a result of constant disruption, I cannot cover a lot of ground in teaching these children. I cannot give the children the amount of attention that they should be getting. I spend so much time trying to settle this child down that it affects teaching time. At times, I feel like there is nothing I can do."

The following excerpts highlight teachers' experience with ODD and CD students, which suggest that ODD and CD students were more disruptive than ADHD students. They caused more bodily harm to their peers and were more disrespectful towards teachers.

When teachers were asked about their experience with ODD or CD students, they described a variety of disruptive behaviour patterns on the part of the ODD or CD child. Whereas, teachers described the behaviours of the ADHD students in terms of out-of-seat activities, the ODD or CD students' behaviours were described in terms of bringing harm to other students. These students would stab other students with pencils, would constantly engage in fights, would be disrespectful to peers and teachers, and would frequently engage in criminal activities such as stealing. Other behaviours included being defiant, playing truant, displaying cruelty to animals, and violating school rules.

Mr C. is one of two males who participated in the research. He has taught for two years and was one of the younger teachers. Mr C. has students with ADHD and with CD. He said he teaches a lower stream [remedial students] class with children who have various learning problems. He related his experience with a CD-affected boy who would fight even without being provoked. If someone just touched him accidentally, he would strike out at the student and was involved in at least three or four fights each week.

Ms F. was quoted earlier talking about her experience with an ADHD student. She teaches two students with ODD and CD. She talked about her experience teaching these two students:

> "This particular boy would beat up students. He would
> hit another child in the head. Every day it is like a boxing
> ring in my class. This boy has beaten up a girl because he
> said the girl "dissed" him. The same student took a broom
> and hit another student in his head."

Ms F. commented on the behaviour pattern of the ODD child by saying, "The ODD boy is very defiant. He goes outside the class without permission."

She recounted an incident with the CD boy:

"One day there was an incident at school and the CD boy took up some stones and began throwing them at the teachers. The teachers had to run."

Mr J. comments on the criminal behaviour of a CD boy he teaches. Mr J. has been teaching for the past eight months. He teaches sixteen-year-old students at the high school level. He presents himself as an innovative young teacher who was certainly not prepared for the student he was about to discuss:

"It is not easy. He likes to be in charge. There was an incident with him recently. Another student told him some guy had taken something from his bag. He immediately went over to the guy, choked, and slapped him in his face. Some boys were making a joke that this student used his hand and boxed a dog and the dog died. He comes to school and tells me all the illegal activities he engages in. When he commits illicit acts outside of school, he comes with the same rage to school."

The teachers accurately stated the behaviour patterns they noted. When compared with DSMIV diagnosis as outlined in chapter 2, the students displayed characteristics consistent with CD.

Ms R.J. also teaches ODD and CD students. She commented on the power struggle that exists between teachers and the OD and CD students:

"Many times these students end up in a power struggle because they do not want the child's behaviour to affect other students. On the other hand, the teachers want respect from the child and the child wants to win the power struggle."

Ms K. described her experience with her ODD student as "horrible". Ms K. appeared somewhat shy and was concerned with how she was going to sound on tape. She jokingly said she would put on her best voice. She became quite serious when the interview began. She commented on her experience with the ODD student:

> "My experience was horrible. When I tried to help this boy, he would not see help as help . . . He would kick at other students; he would openly defy you."

Ms D. is a seasoned teacher. She has been teaching for thirty-eight years. She acts in the capacity of classroom teacher and of principal of the high school where she teaches. She described her experience with a fifteen-year-old boy who was diagnosed with ODD and CD:

> "This boy, he does what he believes is appropriate and conforms to no rules. On some occasions he would display high levels of cruelty to animals."

Although teachers in the study accurately stated characteristics of ODD and CD as outlined in DSMIV, they often did not know what the disorders were, but believed students were just rude with improper home training.

Qualitative Responses on Strategies Teachers Use to Deal with Disruptive Students

Teachers' general reactions to disruptive students were to shout/yell, give a cold stare, give timeout, send to the guidance office, call in parents, use corporal punishment, and ignore or abandon students. These reactions are highlighted in the following quotes:

Ms O. is one of four teachers who described yelling as among one of her reactions to disruptive students:

> "It depends on the day and how many times. I try to keep my cool, repeat my instructions quietly, with a calm tone. Other times I shout 'No!', and ask the child to leave the area."

Ms H. said,

> "I shout, have him stand in a corner, make him sit by himself."

Ms L. said:

> "I would shout at him and say, 'Can't you behave yourself?' I threaten that I am going to send him out of the class, just to see if he would behave himself. I would make him stand outside of the class or give him timeout."

Ms M. said,

> "I shout at him to get back to his seat. I would take him and place him back to his seat."

Teachers responded that they beat or slap. Ms C. is one of three teachers who beat. A number of teachers said they would flog the child if it was not outlawed by the JMOEYC.

Ms C. said,

> "I slap him sometimes. I do not slap him to hurt him but
> just to see if he will stop the behaviour."

Ms G. said her first reaction is to slap the child, but flogging is now
outlawed in Jamaican schools. Instead, she gives the child a stern look.
The look, she said, would help to settle the child for a while:

> "I give him a stern look that will help him settle for
> awhile. I shout at him and ask him to stand away from
> other students."

Ms T. said,

> "I looked at him angrily because he would be tapping,
> tapping on the desk. I also send him out of the class
> sometimes."

Teachers used mostly ad hoc methods to try to control students'
behaviour. Students were often used to run errands and do other menial
tasks in a bid to keep them quiet.

Ms G. said,

> "I give him errands to complete around the classroom.
> I made him an environmental monitor to help keep the
> classroom clean. He cleans the chalkboard."

Ms J. said,

"Depending on what they do at any particular time, they are suspended or punished in some other way, like picking up garbage."

Ms M. said,

"I often give him the responsibility to clean the chalkboard and empty the bin, run errands."

Ms D.C. said,

"I send him to run around the field, go wash his face, or give him the option to do what he wants."

Teachers had more intense reactions towards defiance and conduct-disordered children.

The following comments from teachers highlight the intensity of the reactions. Teachers had more intense reactions towards ODD and CD students than towards students with ADHD. Teachers of ODD—and CD-affected students said that these students would also be suspended. However, none of the seven teachers who taught ADHD students mentioned suspension. Suspension was the course taken more often in the case of the ODD and CD students.

Mr J. talked about his reaction to a student with CD:

"But his behaviour is really bad so the school wants to get rid of him."

Ms. J said,

> "Depending on what they do at any particular time, they are suspended."

Conduct-disordered and ODD students were sent to the principal's office and/or the guidance counsellor's office. Teachers' reactions to CD and ODD students were more intense than their reactions to students with ADHD. For example, Ms F. commented on her reactions to CD:

> "I told the CD boy that he is wicked because he would fight other students."

Mr J teaches both an ADHD-affected student as well as a student affected with both ODD and CD. He commented on his reaction to an ADHD student:

> "That boy is not so bad. I ask him to stand; I give him a lot of work to keep him occupied."

Then Mr J. talked about his reaction to the boy affected with both CD and ODD:

> "They are poisoned with bad behaviour. The boy's behaviour is vulgar and outrageous."

Ms H. commented on her reaction to her CD student:

> "There are times when I will put him in a corner and say, 'Stand and face the wall.'"

Ms J. commented on school action taken against a CD and ODD child:

"Depending on what they do at any particular time, they are suspended or punished in some other way, like picking up garbage. In most of the cases, they are suspended because teachers insist that they are rude to them and they will not teach them."

Ms E. is the only teacher whose reaction is to make a home visit to find out what is happening to her CD student. Ms E. says when she finds a child displaying disruptive behaviours, she makes home visits because she believes that there must be something going on in the home causing the child to behave the way he was behaving.

Positive reactions when behaviour is appropriate:

Teachers described positive reactions to disruptive students when they displayed appropriate behaviours. Four of the twenty teachers described positive reactions and the strategies they use to modify disruptive ADHD students. The following responses from teachers underscore this theme.

Ms O. believed that having an ADHD boy in the class was a good thing because it was a way to teach the children the concept of differences and acceptance:

"There are benefits having a child like that in the class. The other children learn about differences and patience. When the child does something right for the first time they clap."

Ms O. is the only teacher who reasons that it could be beneficial to have a disruptive child in the class.

Ms R. described her feelings of frustration with having an ADHD boy in her class. She commented on a strategy she used to help the student cope with his problem. Ms R. is one of two teachers who use this strategy:

> "Probably twice during the morning, I would give him a break apart from the water break and bathroom breaks all the students get. I would ask him if he wants to run around the field; and so quite often, he would run around the field and back. I would give him timeout."

By "timeout", Ms R. meant time to release some of his energy so that he would not be so disruptive, but she explained that this was not the timeout given as a behaviour modification strategy. She commented further: "There was lots of praise for him when he did do something good."

Ms T. also has a reward system in place. She commented:

> "I have a system of rewards, that if he finishes his work he will be rewarded. I give him praise and ask the entire class to clap him [to applaud him for his good work] . . . I leave him in charge of the class. When I do this, he keeps in check. I try and encourage him to do his work."

Ms T. also described a token system that she has in place to reward good behaviour. The child's parent also was involved in this and would reward him at home for his good behaviour.

Mr C. devised the strategy of giving his ADHD students activities in a "short burst", meaning that he gave the student work to do according to the child's short attention span:

"Well, I believe that because of the disorder they are experiencing, they need special activities to do. So I give activities in short bursts instead of giving them work for an hour or forty-five minutes."

Ms G. highlighted the strategy she was planning use to help modify the behaviours of the disruptive students in her class:

"What I am trying to do is get a dance class going so that these children can channel their fighting energy. I have also a session where students come in and talk to me about the problems they are having."

For the most part, teachers' reaction and strategies were unfocused and in reaction to how the student's behaviour was making them feel. This left them angry and frustrated about the efforts they were making without results.

CHAPTER 3

Understanding the Importance of Medication as a Treatment Option

This chapter is primarily to help teachers understand that disruptive behaviour does have a biological basis; and treatment options may include medication. The issue with understanding medication use is that often children with ADHD may need medication to be able to stay calm in order to benefit from classroom instructions. This chapter also sensitizes the reader about Jamaican parents' resistance to medicating children.

The use of psychotropic medication in the treatment of ADHD has been widely debated. The debate is whether children diagnosed with ADHD should receive medication or use alternative treatments. Some argue that children should not receive medication because of the many side effects. Another school of thought is that these medications often are addictive. Some African-Americans and African-Caribbean persons argue against medicating children. They tend to argue that the medication causes more harm than alternative methods used to treat the disorders.

An investigation into aetiology of ADHD implicates environmental factors. According to Vollmer (2000), children who grow up in chaotic environments often have difficulty regulating attention and impulsivity.

Also implicated, is the role that emotionally-charged environmental factors play in the aetiology of ADHD. Behaviours seen in children with ADHD are not simply the result of environmental factors, or some sort of distortion of perception on the part of parents and teachers, but rather a very real brain dysfunction. In ADHD, Vollmer's (2004) research revealed dysfunction of the prefrontal subcortical system, often with greater involvement of areas of the right hemisphere.

The debate goes further to argue that if environmental factors contribute, it therefore means that appropriate behaviour modification techniques can be a treatment option. How then do we differentiate between environmental aetiology and biological aetiology of the disorder? It makes sense that medication, along with behaviour modification techniques, be the treatment modalities of choice.

The Jamaican school situation indicates that a large number of students present with symptoms of ADHD (Pottinger 2001). Pottinger notes that while properly designed studies have not been conducted to identify the rate of ADHD in Jamaica, small samples have shown that about 15–25 per cent of Jamaicans are affected by ADHD. The area of concern lies with, since a number of Jamaicans are suffering from the disorder, what is the ideal form of treatment for these individuals. Many Jamaicans are sceptics when it involves medicating children. Many Jamaican parents believe that it is an unwise practice to medicate children with psychotropic medications. They also believe that ADHD is a label psychiatrists have found to excuse rude behaviours especially on the part of children. This has led many Jamaican parents to refuse to medicate their children with ADHD, who then go untreated, become disruptive to the school system, and do not achieve their potential.

It is believed that many children in the US who are diagnosed with ADHD are over–medicated. Some argue that not enough is being done to seek alternative treatment for ADHD. How effective is psychotropic treatment of ADHD? Are alternative treatments comparable to psychotropic, or better? If parents and other stakeholders were able to understand the indications and contraindications of ADHD, along with medication and its effectiveness or non-effectiveness, parents might be able to make informed decisions about treatment for their children. The effectiveness of alternative treatment would also help to provide information to aid them in making decisions that will benefit their children. If parents lack this knowledge, effective treatment for children with ADHD will be grossly undermined.

History of Psychopharmacology and ADHD

The disorder ADHD has gone through several name changes. The disorder was first identified in 1902 and referred to as Morbid Defects of Moral Control. In 1922, it was renamed Post Encephalitic Behaviour Disorder. By 1960, it had seen another name change to Minimal Brain Dysfunction, and in 1968, renamed Hyperkinetic Reaction (Cipkala-Gaffin 1998). The term ADHD was first used in 1980 and is one of the most widely research disorders (Cipkala-Gaffin 1998).

Medication for treatment of ADHD began in the 1930s, with the use of amphetamines as first line treatment. In 1956, the Food and Drug Administration approved Ritalin. The drug, Adderal, gained approval in 1996; and by 1999 Concerta was the new drug of choice for ADHD. Later that year, Metadata gained FDA approval. In 2001 and 2002 the drugs Focalin and Strattera gained FDA approval as another ADHD treatment. In Jamaica in recent years, Concerta is the drug most recommended by pharmaceutical companies and most widely prescribed by child psychiatrists.

Assessing the Efficacy of Psychotropics in the Treatment of ADHD

Psychotropic medications remain the treatment of choice for ADHD (Madaan 2008). Pharmacological intervention helps in the reduction of core symptoms of ADHD, thus helping the child to function in various settings that call for staying focused and in control of impulses. Several researches have addressed the safety and effectiveness of ADHD pharmacotherapy (Madaan 2008). Current pharmacotherapies that have proven efficacious are methylphenidate, amphetamines, and atomoxetine (Madaan 2008). Dexamfetamine, as a treatment for ADHD, is on the increase and is an efficacious treatment option. As well, third line agents such as TCAs (tricyclic antidepressants) are in use in the treatment of ADHD (Graham & Coghill 2008).

Over the years, medication for the treatment of ADHD has been on the increase. In the United Kingdom, prescriptions for stimulant medication rose from 183,000 in 1991 to 1.58 million in 1995. There was a four-fold increase in the US between 1987 and 1996 (Graham & Coghill 2008). Similarly, in Jamaica there has been a rise in the use of medication for the treatment of ADHD (Bernard 2011). This increase is because of the increase in psychologists in Jamaica who are now diagnosing more cases of the disorder. In Jamaica, in the past, children presenting with the symptoms of ADHD would go under-diagnosed and were seen as being rude.

As more children receive a diagnosis of ADHD in Jamaica, the question of efficacy of medication use arises and the cultural dictates involving child medication become evident. Studies have revealed that use of immediate-release or short-acting stimulants twice daily may reduce symptoms (Madaan, et al. 2008). The application of the osmotic controlled release oral delivery system used in concerto provides twelve-hour duration of action for methylphenidate. The methylphenidate patch has proven effective because of its closing properties. Lisdexamfetamine provides a good option for patients who have ADHD comorbid with substance abuse. Although ADHD medications have proven efficacious in reducing symptoms, they are not without adverse effects. An understanding of these adverse effects would help physicians to prescribe appropriately and minimize possible side effects.

ADHD medications do have side effects but, studies have proven that medications for ADHD have only mild and minor adverse effects in most cases (Graham & Coghill 2008). There are two categories of ADHD medications, stimulant and non-stimulants. However, there has been a paucity of research in effects of stimulant psychopharmatherapies for ADHD (Graham & Coghill 2008). ADHD medication, taken according to specification, is usually safe with few side effects; and side effects may be mild as well as serious, although serious side effects are rare (Graham & Coghill). These researchers conducted Meta analysis on the adverse effects of ADHD psychopharmatherapies and results indicated that stimulant side effects include loss of appetite, sleep problems, stomach pains, and headaches. Common side effects of atomoxetine include abdominal pain; decreased appetite; nausea, and vomiting; early morning awakening; irritability and mood swings; and increased heart rate.

A study conducted by Scheffler (2009) suggests that children given stimulants to treat ADHD score higher on math and reading tests than children with the condition who were not on medication. The study tracked 594 children diagnosed with ADHD from kindergarten through to fifth grade who were on Ritalin and Adderall. These students performed better on standardized tests than peers with ADHD who were not on any medication.

The National Institute of Mental Health (NIMH) carried out an in-depth study of ADHD treatment, called the Multimodal Treatment Study of Children with ADHD. The study showed that Ritalin is effective in treating the symptoms of ADHD either alone or in combination with behavioural therapy; and that medication alone was more effective than behavioural therapy alone. The NIMH studies reported that ADHD medications are safe to take and are very effective. The study also demonstrated that a combination of medication and behavioural therapy was very effective in helping students with ADHD, thus making teachers and parents less stressed in dealing with the symptoms of ADHD.

Cultural View of Medication as the First Line Treatment for ADHD: Jamaican Context

In Jamaica, a child diagnosed with ADHD raises the question for most parents about what treatment options are available. In my practice as a psychologist, depending on the severity of the ADHD, when parents review the options and medication is one of them, a significant number of parents refuse this option. In Jamaica, the reality is that a shortage of individuals with the expertise to use alternative treatment such as, behavioural therapy or computer-based therapy exists. Therefore, it is important to determine why parents are averse to medicating their children, and what the available alternatives in Jamaica are for the treatment of ADHD.

That their child is susceptible to addiction is a foremost concern of parents. According to the National Institute on Drug Abuse (NIMH), children who use ADHD medication are less likely to have problems with substance abuse. If taken as prescribed, medication can improve the symptoms of ADHD and the likelihood of addiction is a remote possibility. Many Jamaican parents do not believe in medicating children with psychotropic drugs; and, therefore, they believe that there is the likelihood that these medications could induce psychosis. Many parents in Jamaica would be comfortable using alternative treatment such as dietary changes and herbal supplements rather than to use pharmacological drugs. The use of herbal supplements is steeped in the Jamaican culture. The use of herbs is rooted in an era when slaves relied heavily on herbal products, a legacy derived from West Africa, the home of slaves who came to Jamaica. The use of herbal treatment appears appealing rather than psychotropic medication for many Jamaican parents.

The Efficacy of Alternative Treatments

If Jamaican parents continue to be reluctant to use medication as a first line treatment for ADHD, exploration of efficacious alternative treatments is indicated. Parents should be aware that there is no cure for ADHD at this time (NIMH 2009). Some of the alternative treatments include behavioural therapy and computer-based therapy. According to NIMH, alternative treatments include special diets, herbal supplements, homeopathic treatments, vision therapy, chiropractic adjustments, yeast infection treatments, anti-motion sickness medication, metronome training, auditory stimulation, applied kinesiology (realigning bones in the skull), and brain wave biofeedback. The National Institute of Drug Addiction comments that rigorous scientific research has not found alternatives to be effective in managing the symptoms of ADHD (NIMH 2009). According to NIMH, psychosocial/behavioural treatment such as social skills training, or individual therapies have not proven effective as medicine for the core systems of ADHD. However, recommendations are that behavioural treatment be used as the initial treatment if the ADHD symptoms are mild. Studies have shown that a combination of behavioural therapy and medication can result in a lower dosage of medication and significant reduction in symptoms (NIMH 2009). When behavioural treatment is used, both teachers and parents should attend workshops designed to teach them behavioural strategies that will help children attend and stay focused. The behaviour programme should include rewards for good behaviour and consequences for unwanted behaviours.

Optimal Arousal Theory

The theory postulates that each individual must have an optimal level of arousal to improve academic performance. Children with ADHD can reach their optimal performance level with the use of bright colours to highlight difficult parts of words. The use of brightly-coloured mats to do homework is another way to sustain the attention of children with ADHD. Rock music can be distracting for some persons, but has proven useful, when played in the background while ADHD children are studying. According to Cripe, 1986, the rhythmic beat in rock music increases nervous system arousal, the music masks other distractions, reduces tension, thus reducing overall motor activity. The study concluded that ADHD students who participated in the study showed improved performance while listening to rock music.

Why Teachers Need to Know about Medication

Dealing with disruptive behaviours in the classroom is often frustrating to teachers. They often use some kind of behavioural intervention that does not seem to work, hence, increasing their frustration. Teachers need to understand that a multimodal approach is the best way to deal with disruptive behaviours. Teachers need to know that medication is an option in treating ADHD. They also need to know that medication does not necessarily eliminate behavioural problems, but often reduces disruptive behaviour. A child on medication makes it easier for the teacher to implement behavioural strategies. Medication does not always work, so a child may be on medication and behavioural problems persist. Some medication, depending on what the child is on, may interfere with learning. More medication does not necessarily mean better behaviour.

A combination of low-dose medication and behaviour modification has proven more efficacious than higher doses as the only treatment option.

Parents should notify teachers if their child is on medication. Teachers help to monitor how well behaviours have changed; or, perhaps, even though the child is on medication, remain unchanged. The teacher can provide feedback to parents on how well the child is behaving since the introduction of medication or a change in dosage. Another situation that teachers need to be aware of is that not every child with ADHD is a good candidate for medication. This is because some children have adverse reactions to the ADHD medication. In that case, a more comprehensive behaviour modification programme is recommended.

Teachers are usually part of the assessment process. Teachers do not diagnose ADHD, but help psychiatrists and psychologists rate the child's behaviour on standardized instruments. It is important that teachers rate behaviours accurately in terms of mild, moderate, or severe, as this could greatly assist a psychiatrist to determine if medication is a treatment option. Teachers do not, in any form or shape, make mention of the child being on medication in a classroom setting, as this would constitute unprofessional conduct. The information about a child on medication is to help the teacher carry out their task from a place of understanding and professionalism that will help a special needs child reach his potential.

Medication for Oppositional Defiant Disorder and Conduct Disorder

No drug has been approved to treat ODD and CD. Oppositional Defiant Disorder and Conduct Disorder are often comorbid with other disruptive disorders or mental disorders. These disorders could include anxiety and depression. Medication is usually given to treat the related disorders. Drugs that may be prescribed to treat ODD symptoms include:

a. Stimulant for ADHD,

b. Methylphenidate (Ritalin),

c. Dextroamphetamine (Dexedrine),

d. Antidepressants for depression or anxiety (Lexapro),

e. Fluoxetine (Prozac),

f. Resperidone (Risperdal),

g. Aripiprazole (Abilify).

It is recommended that medication should not be a stand-alone treatment. Medication in combination with psychotherapy and behaviour modification strategies at home and school is the ideal treatment option.

Stimulants, antidepressants, lithium, anticonvulsants and clonidine have all been used in the treatment of conduct disorder. Stimulants, (Ritalin) are the most-used treatment for conduct disorder. The efficacy of the stimulants for the treatment of CD has not been established. Antidepressants such as Wellbutrin and Fluoxetine (Prozac) have been known to produce significant reduction in impulsive and aggressive behaviour. The selective serotonin reuptake inhibitors (SSRIs) may be helpful in treating children with conduct disorder and comorbid major depression.

Future Trends

As more and more children present with ADHD there is going to be a need for appropriate treatment modality. There are a number of myths surrounding ADHD. A widely-known myth is that children can outgrow ADHD symptoms by the teenage years. It has been proven that this not the case. Children do not outgrow ADHD symptoms, but some of the symptoms may diminish over time. Although some may outgrow the symptoms, the majority remains symptomatic. Fifty per cent of children with ADHD have symptoms into later adulthood (Fornarotto & O'Connell 2002). It appears that medication will continue to be the first line treatment modality. Attention Deficit Hyperactivity Disorder is one of the most widely-researched disorders. As more research is available, more data will become available and more treatment options explored. More research will be conducted on current alternative treatments and their efficacy in treating the disorder. More knowledge will be available to parents and counsellors, so best treatment decisions will provide efficacious results for children diagnosed with ADHD.

It is very important that teachers are aware that medication is part of the treatment option for ADHD so that when behavioural modification technique seem not to work, it is likely that a medication will be the first-line treatment

Summary

The purpose of this chapter was to explore the use of medication and examine alternative treatment for ADHD. It also explored prevailing cultural views of medication in the Jamaican context. Medication is the first line of treatment for ADHD. Several studies point to the conclusion that ADHD medications are efficacious. Attention Deficit Hyperactivity Disorder medications do have side effects but they are usually few, mild and minor. Studies show that the benefits of using ADHD medication far outweigh the side effects. The medications have proved efficacious in reducing symptoms of impulsivity, hyperactivity, and inattention. There are alternative treatments, which include both behavioural therapy, and dietary and herbal supplements. Behavioural therapies are efficacious but not so much as medication in the treatment of ADHD. A combination of behavioural therapy and medication has proven to be effective by reducing dosage and significantly reducing symptoms.

Dietary and herbal supplements have not proven to be effective but no definitive studies have proven the effectiveness of diet or herbal supplements as an effective treatment for ADHD. Many Jamaican parents do not want to use medication as a first line treatment because they believe medicating children with psychotropic could induce mental disorders. They also believe that ADHD medication can be addictive. They tend to believe in the use of herbal supplements because of cultural factors.

The implication of the findings is that Jamaican children with ADHD may be going untreated because of cultural factors affecting the use of medication. Medications have proven efficacious in the treatment of ADHD. Herbal supplements and dietary changes have not yet been fully researched. It, therefore, will necessitate that psychoeducation be undertaken to help Jamaican parents understand that medication can not only be quite effective, but can help to reduce symptoms. Behavioural interventions have proven to be efficacious, but lack of qualified personnel in the Jamaican context makes this approach not readily available. The need for psychoeducation in appropriate treatment modalities for the treatment of ADHD becomes imperative.

CHAPTER 4

Strategies Teachers Can Use to Deal with ADHD, ODD, and CD Students

The research I conducted revealed that teachers admitted they did not understand how to deal with these students and were often overwhelmed trying to teach a child with one or both of these disorders. The study showed that teachers' responses were characterized by an absence of any coordinated plan or strategies based on research or knowledge about the problem. Teachers' general reactions were to shout, yell, give a cold stare, give timeout, send the child to the guidance office, call in the parents, use corporal punishment, and ignore or abandon students. Teachers often used ad hoc methods to try to control students' behaviour and displayed positive attitudes towards students when students displayed appropriate behaviours. Because they had no knowledge of the disorders, the teachers did not have the ability to adequately address the problems presented by these students. An ecosystem approach is advised in order to address the needs of students who present with disruptive behaviour disorder. This approach looks at the individual as part of a system that is interconnected and interrelated. This approach would involve psychologists, teachers, parents, social workers, and the family system.

Psychological intervention would include appropriate assessment, accurate diagnosis, and treatment planning. Parental involvement would include providing psychoeducation, parenting education and parenting skills with training in behaviour modification techniques. Teachers would also need psychoeducation, which could lead them towards developing skills of reframing and self-reflection and developing behaviour modification techniques to aid in shaping appropriate classroom behaviours. Social work intervention would address social needs of the child to ensure appropriate resources are available to the child and family. The model of intervention is illustrated in Figure 1.

ECOSYSTEM APPROACH TO MANAGING
DISRUPTIVE BEHAVIOURS

> Psychologically
> Assessment
> &
> Diagnosis

Intervention Strategies Including

Psychologists	Teachers	Parents

Psychologists	Teachers	Parents

Psychological Intervention Placed in Therapy
• Individual
• Group
• Family
	Teachers:
	Reframing
	Self Reflection
	Behavior modification
	  Strategies
		Group therapy
		Family therapy
		Monthly Parents
		Meeting
		Parenting workshop
		Application of behaviour
		  modification

Educational • Special Schools • Inclusive intervention	Social Worker–address social needs • After school activities	Psychiatrist— medication—moderate to severe disruptive behaviours. Monitor for compliance side effects

This chapter is primarily concerned with strategies that teachers can employ to help students who present with ADHD, CD, or ODD. Some experts contend that the first step in managing problem behaviours in class is self-reflection on the part of the teacher. A crucial factor in the success of classroom interventions is the teacher's belief that students are capable of acting appropriately. Teachers convey positive expectations by involving students in setting up classroom rules, by clearly publishing rules for behaviour, and above all, by rewarding good behaviour. Although there is some controversy about the use of extrinsic rewards in class (which critics argue diminishes intrinsic motivation), there is unanimous support for the use of praise and positive feedback.

One thing that teachers are typically unaware of is that their own behaviour can trigger outbursts from students with disruptive behaviour disorders. Much of the power of self-reflection is due to its ability to defuse conflict. According to Richardson & Shupe (2003), teachers who are cognizant of their own emotional processes are more likely to reduce classroom conflicts such as power struggles with students. In addition to understanding the way their behaviour affects students, teachers must be aware of the various contexts in which problem behaviours occur at the beginning of class, at the end of the class, or as the weekend approaches.

According to Palardy and Palardy (1987, p. 89) "Knowing when the problem times are is an important first step in planning to prevent them". In essence, adopting a proactive approach is the best strategy for averting problem behaviour. Self-management strategy includes teachers teaching students with behaviour disorders how to self monitor. Emphasizing the vital importance of creating a positive learning environment, Jenson et al. (2004, p.72) state that, "Self-management strategies are some of the most effective approaches for students with externalizing disorders to influence the 'postiveness' of their academic environment."

Elements of self-management programmes include self-monitoring and self-evaluation as well as techniques designed to elicit positive feedback and praise from teachers. Self-management strategies help teachers gain a sense of self-efficacy by allowing them to feel in control of their behaviour and its outcomes. Teachers find self-management strategies are effective for increasing engagement and decreasing disruptive behaviour in students with ADHD (Reis 2002).

Self-Reflection on the Part of the Teacher

1. Do you have a child in your class diagnosed with ODD, CD or ADHD? Have you considered the reason for the child's problem behaviour? If there is no diagnosis, do you understand that the disruptive behaviour may be a manifestation of one of the behavioural disorders? Do you know what you should do if you suspect that a child's behavioural pattern is disruptive?

2. What are the behaviours that this child exhibits in the classroom? Are you able to identify the characteristics of a behavioural disorder? Do you label a student rather than understand the cause and purpose of the behaviour?

3. How does the child's behaviour affect classroom functioning? This question challenges your understanding of how the behaviour affects classroom functions and your awareness, so that appropriate strategies can be put in place.

4. When the child is being disruptive, how do you normally react? This question seeks to capture your reaction to disruptive behaviours. Are you reacting because of how the behaviour is making you feel, or based on knowledge of reasons for the disruption?

5. How do you feel about children who disrupt classroom activities? Are you feeling disgusted, and if so, why? Do you know why you are feeling this way?

6. When children are so disruptive, what action should be taken against these children? Do you understand the appropriate actions that should be taken against these students?

7. How do you normally cope with disruptive behaviour? Are you aware of coping strategies you can use in the classroom?

8. What do you believe the school should do about students who present with ODD, CD or ADHD? Are you aware of appropriate measures to be taken to assist these students, and if there are structures in place to deal with these behaviours? Do you have knowledge of behaviour modification strategies? Moreover, do you know how to implement them?

9. How seriously do you view behaviours displayed by children with disruptive ADHD? Do you have an understanding of that student's behaviour problems and that this may be a disorder that needs professional assistance?

Reframing

Another approach teachers may need to take is reframing, which is a key element of the ecosystem approach. Reframing is a method that allows teachers, when faced with problem behaviour, to ask themselves a series of questions designed to neutralize issues of blame and to focus on finding new solutions to problems. The teacher could ask a series of questions to help put the problem behaviour in a new frame in order to find workable solutions.

- Do I understand and know what is causing the behaviour?
- Is the child on medication? Did the child take the medication? Is medication noncompliance exacerbating the behaviour?

- Did I give the break that the child was slated to have at twenty-minute intervals?
- What measures can I quickly put in place to ensure the student settles down?

These and other questions are part of a reframing exercise to bring about a solution rather than to assign blame on a student or yourself. This approach is consistent with the idea that positive communication is the key to altering problem behaviour.

Behaviour Modification Techniques

Assertive Discipline: Strategies to Help Students with CD and ODD

Because teachers are typically unaware that their own behaviour can trigger an outburst from students with disruptive behaviour disorder, there may be power struggles in the classroom as a result. Behaviours that teachers should avoid displaying include openly threatening students. Students with CD or ODD try to test the limits of the teacher. When teachers threaten, the students will dare the teacher to carry out the threat and may want to become physical. Teachers should always bear in mind that the behaviour patterns displayed by these students are a manifestation of a disorder that is often outside their control. As a result, teachers should never threaten students; this will only add to the power struggle. Another behaviour that should definitely be avoided is responding to CD or ODD students in a sarcastic manner or getting angry. The child with ODD may set out to annoy and irritate others, but getting angry is exactly the response they are trying to elicit from the teachers, since the child wants to engage in confrontation and to assert power. Getting the teacher angry serves the purpose of the ODD student and proves the teacher is not in control. This may result in the teacher losing face with the student and their peers.

Teachers should avoid confronting students in the presence of their peers. ODD or CD children who believe that a teacher is embarrassing them in front of peers will want to save face and will retaliate by excessively annoying the teacher or by becoming vindictive. The CD student may introduce physical violence or take revenge by slashing a teacher's tyre or act out by using other antisocial behaviour.

Teachers should avoid responding too quickly, for a quick response may only exacerbate the situation and may not be appropriate. This is a good time for the teacher to STOP, THINK and ACT by using the reframing technique; this will result in a self-controlled response.

Teachers make a fundamental mistake when interacting with CD or ODD students by letting the interaction continue for too long a time. Remaining in the interaction too long will lead to the teacher's losing control of the situation. If the student refuses to comply with a request, the teacher may engage the student in a back and forth discourse that will go nowhere. This situation should be avoided; the teacher is the one who must interact with the child even though the student continues to defy him/her.

An example of engaging a student in a situation for too long is demonstrated by the following: When a teacher asked an ODD student for his homework, the young man handed in his book without the homework. The teacher continued to ask for the homework, and the student continued to say he had handed in the homework. This back and forth interaction between teacher and student continued for almost fifteen minutes until the ODD student got up and locked the classroom and held onto the teacher. The interaction continued until a student ran to the principal's office for help. The principal arrived and told the young man to go to see the coach, who gave him several push-ups to do because of his behaviour. This is a classic mistake in the handling of such a case. The appropriate way to have handled this incident was to collect the student's book, even though no homework was inside; and then, after class, talk with the student about the challenges he may be facing in completing the assignment. The teacher could find out from the student how best to assist him in completing homework.

Another mistake teachers may make is to bribe students. Teachers should never bribe CD or ODD students. Bribing in this sense is "I will give you this, if you do that." This kind of transaction usually backfires because CD or ODD students often lack empathy for others, and if the situation deteriorates, the student will lay blame on the teacher.

A teacher should not spend time trying to convince CD or ODD students to do something, for they are often oppositional and defiant and breaking rules may give them pleasure. A better approach is to allow the students to recognise that they have an option to complete the teacher's request or they will face the consequences. Teachers never belittle students, because this will only further increase oppositional and defiant behaviour and exacerbate conduct problems. These students already feel that nobody cares. They face, on a daily basis, a barrage of negative comments due to their problematic behaviour patterns. If the student is belittled, this only validates what he/she is already feeling and only serves to increase a maladaptive behaviour pattern.

Strategies that May Diminish Power Struggles in the Classroom

When a CD or ODD student is being disruptive, provide simple directives or choices, and stick to them. For example, "John, please be seated or go to the detention hall;" or, "I understand your concern, but please wait until the end of our discussion. Then, I will deal with your concerns." Some teachers will argue that this is easier said than done. True, but teachers should allow students to feel that the teachers are the allies of the children and whatever they are saying is in the best interests of their students.

It is very important that teachers identify problem behaviours in the classroom and develop some pre-determined consequences. Students should be involved in rule setting and consequences, so that they are aware that certain behaviours generate certain results. For example, CD students who are caught stealing, breaking school property, or harassing others, should already have been given clearly-stated consequences for such behaviours. These consequences should be consistently applied and should be irksome enough to make the students want to conform by modifying their behaviour. For the CD child, such consequences may mean the child is placed in a residential facility that caters to boys/girls with conduct problems or who have broken the law. There should be more structured residential settings and other such facilities geared towards rehabilitation of children with serious conduct problems.

Teachers should carefully listen to the student before responding. If the teacher does not truly understand what the student wants or needs, a simple situation could escalate into something huge. One teacher in the study mentioned that a young boy took the bag belonging to a boy presenting with CD. Before the teacher listened to what had really happened, he was told to sit down. Because of this simple incident, there was a big uproar in the school, and the entire school became involved. A teacher should avoid getting caught up in a disruptive student's manipulative schemes.

When giving instructions to these students, do so in a calm tone and make instructions brief and very direct. This will prevent the student from finding loopholes for an argument with the teacher. Another important strategy is to discuss the problem privately with the student. This shows the students that you have their best interests at heart and that you want them to succeed. You do not want a situation to arise in class that may escalate into something you will not be able to control or walk away from before it reaches boiling point.

As you self-reflect, think about your current behaviour patterns that lock you into power struggles with students. Instead, have a one-on-one discussion with your CD or ODD student. During this discussion show that you understand; and clearly outline, appropriate behaviours that are desired for your CD or ODD students. Identify behaviours they display that can be ignored, since often these behaviours are displayed to gain attention.

Attend to CD and ODD students when they are engaged in the desired behaviour by quickly whispering praise and identifying the behaviour for which they are being praised. Seek opportunities to channel their energies into doing useful acts of kindness to others. Teachers should always remember that a team effort is needed. You are a part of a team, one link in the team who helps these students succeed despite their behavioural problems. There are going to be times when you cannot help, but another member of the team should be in place. Students who present with CD or ODD can be quite stressful to teach. You should take time out to ensure that you practice stress management techniques that will help you cope.

The ADHD Student

Although teachers may find teaching ADHD children to be annoying and frustrating, a professional attitude towards them should be, "What can I do to help this child keep focused?" Well, teachers, there are a number of things that you can do to help your ADHD students. You must remember that the primary difficulties for ADHD are hyperactivity, inattention, and impulsivity. Hyperactive children have problems with distractibility, an inability to pay attention to and control that to which they pay attention. They are unable to inhibit their response to distractions, noise, movement, or their own inner thoughts.

In helping students with ADHD, a teacher must again focus on their knowledge base of the disorder, their characteristics and teaching style. Teacher's knowledge is a key factor in helping students with ADHD. The teacher must know that ADHD students can be inconsistent in their behaviour. They may succeed one day in completing tasks, which may lead the teacher to believe that they are capable of completing this task all the time. This is not so, students with ADHD are inconsistent. This knowledge will help teachers refrain from calling ADHD students lazy. Rather than criticise or embarrass, teachers need to guide the process so that students are motivated to learn.

Teachers' characteristics that foster good teaching and learning include flexibility and sensitivity. Flexibility means the teacher does not expect that all students will perform or complete tasks in the same manner. The flexible teacher understands the unique needs of her students and responds with this in mind. Sensitive teachers never berate or openly confront students. Teachers, your goal is to build students' self-esteem, not to tear it down.

Teachers need to be mindful to consider a number of factors when dealing with students with ADHD. These factors include the classroom setting, the child, and what you are bringing to the teaching/learning experience. Teachers should consider classroom accommodation, reinforcement strategies, and well-timed consequences for infringements.

Classroom Accommodations

A teacher may seat the ADHD child close to her and away from doors or windows to limit distractions, or have the child face the teacher at closer range. Look for signs of restlessness; give a nonverbal cue to stay on task or offer a pat on their shoulder to remind the child to take a quick break from work. Teachers may wish to experiment with music. Some students may benefit from music after recess and lunch to calm the class down. ADHD students could benefit from earphones to provide them with instructions and limit distractions. The work area of the ADHD student should be free from distractions. Use a variety of visual, auditory and kinaesthetic lessons to sustain attention.

Short lesson periods using a variety of pacing helps the ADHD student stay focused. The ADHD child displays immature social behaviour, so use positive reinforcement; this will limit their use of negative behaviour to gain attention. Ideally, there should be a teacher's aide to do one-on-one sessions with the ADHD student.

Teacher-Centred Approaches

The teacher should practice reframing, as a psychological intervention. This will help the teacher build an alliance with the disruptive student and to help the student feel understood. It is important that the teacher develops a psychological contract with students. This psychological contract could be a written agreement with the student that spells out that the teacher is willing to assist the student to ensure he/she stays on task.

Secret signals can be developed and shared to signal if the student is feeling restless. The teacher should then look for signs of restlessness and give the student a cue to stay on task or take a break. Positive reinforcement will get positive results. The teacher needs to notice when the student is doing good, and voice a positive reaction in order to reduce attention-seeking behaviours. Because ADHD students have problems following instructions, teachers should use specific, brief, and personal instructions, written down so they acts as a reminder to be on task. Since these students have problems with impulsivity, teachers should teach them how to STOP, THINK, AND ACT. Paste rules on the child's test as a reminder to stay on task. The teacher may place a special card on their desk as a reminder for appropriate behaviour. These cards remind a student to raise her/his hand before speaking. Teachers should also provide five—to ten-minute warnings for a student before implementing a punishment. Give the child a chance to self-regulate. Instead of sending the child out of classroom because he/she left their seat, provide alternative behaviour to help them deal with an impulsive urge. Ask the student to take a brief break, designate an area in the classroom called a "calming down area", and then have them return to their seat after the impulsive urge has passed. You might ask the student to remember the rule on the table, which says they should raise their hand before they speak, or the class will wait for silence before continuing. By providing alternative behaviour, you have the chance to instruct your students, such as "This is a moment that I want you to STOP, THINK & ACT. Check your feelings and decide what you want to do, bearing in mind the consequence for your action." Again, the teacher could say, "You are allowed to move quietly to the side, back or front of the class," and remind the student to take a deep breath.

The American Academy of Pediatrics and CHADD, offer tips on how teachers can best help students with ADD/ADHD:

1. Display classroom rules. Classroom rules must be very clear and concise.

2. Provide clear and concise instructions for academic assignments.

3. Break complex instructions into small parts.

4. Show students how to use an assignment book to keep track of their homework and daily assignments.

5. Post a daily schedule and homework assignments in the same place each day.

6. Tape a copy on the child's desk.

7. Plan academic subjects for the morning hours.

8. Explain to the student what to do to avoid negative consequences.

9. Reward target behaviours immediately and continuously. Use negative consequences only after a positive reinforcement program has had enough time to become effective.

10. Deliver negative consequences in a firm, business-like way without emotion, lectures, or long-winded explanations.

11. Deal with disruptions with as little interruption as possible. When teachers have classroom disruptions, it is imperative that these are dealt with immediately and with as little interruption of your class momentum as possible. If students are talking amongst themselves while the teacher is having a classroom discussion, ask one of the students who is committing an infringement a question to try to get him/her back on track. Teachers can get a noise meter that produces a ringing sound if noise levels are exceeded. If you have to stop your teaching time to deal with disruptions, you are robbing students who want to learn during their precious in-class time.

Teachers should try to avoid confrontations in front of students at all costs, because wherever there is a confrontation in class, there is going to be a winner and a loser. Obviously, the teacher has the responsibility of keeping order and discipline in the class. However, it is prudent to deal with disciplinary issues in private rather than to cause a student to be embarrassed in front of her/his peers. It is not a good idea to make an example out of a disciplinary issue. Even though other students get the point, you may lose any chance of actually teaching that student anything in your class. Teachers should use their best judgment to determine which behaviours to ignore. Stop disruptions with a little humour. Sometimes all it takes is to break the ice by having a good laugh to get things back on track in a classroom. An education officer reported that while she was a classroom teacher, a boy looked at her and said that her face was very oily. The teacher's response was that she had stopped selling oil to Texaco, and this is why she was generating so much oil in her face. The class had a good laugh and the student became silent without further interruptions. Many times, however, teachers confuse good humour with sarcasm. While humour can quickly diffuse a situation, sarcasm may harm your relationship with the students involved. Use your best judgment but realize that what some people think as funny others find to be offensive.

Over Plan, Avoid Information Overload

Free time is something teachers should avoid. By allowing students time to talk each day when lessons end too early for the allotted period, you are setting a precedent about how you view the teaching and learning process and your subject. In order to avoid this situation, teachers should over plan. When you have too much to cover, you will never run out of lessons, and you will avoid free time. However, it is important to note how to avoid information overload. Take into consideration the ADHD student's attention span, vary the length of the work, and break work into small segments.

Reinforcement Strategies, Selecting Appropriate Consequences

Reinforcement and consequences are key components in managing ADHD students' behaviour. Teachers should carefully design rewards and consequences to meet each ADHD child's needs. The approach of "one size fits all" may not work. Children with ADHD require consequences that are more positive. Negative verbal consequences, like reprimanding, results in embarrassment and erodes self-esteem. Use only mild punishment such as timeout. This, too, should be used with caution because if used inappropriately, it could prove ineffective. Timeout may be used primarily to control acting-out behaviour and failure to comply. Teachers need to be sure and distinguish between noncompliance and misunderstanding of instructions due to inattention. It would be wise to be clear before effecting timeout. Teacher, use your discretion when giving timeout. The time given does not necessarily have to match the student's age. Do not overuse, as students will misbehave to get timeout. Ensure that the student is devoid of stimulation for the period of timeout but must return to a stimulating activity. Use soft reprimands by quietly talking to the student so others cannot hear.

Teachers, deliver reinforcements immediately after the desired behaviour to ensure the child knows that the reward is for that specific behaviour. Rewards should be age-appropriate (Figure 1.2)

Figure 1.2 Classroom Rewards

1. No homework day
2. Pats, hugs, touch on the hand
3. Extra time at recess
4. Running errands
5. Dining with the teacher—this could be a group activity
6. Use of headphone
7. Leaving class early for lunch
8. Tutoring another child
9. Helping in the administrative office
10. Cleaning the chalkboard
11. Using a computer
12. Using videotape to present a lesson

Teachers, carefully select consequences for infringements. Consequences are more effective when given immediately and often enough to become irksome to the student. The aim is to reduce or eliminate the undesirable behaviour. ADHD students are used to negative reinforcement. Usually they are constantly criticized and given negative attention. According to many experts in behaviour modification it is important to give more positive attention; that is, attend to students when they are behaving appropriately. Interestingly, in using positive attention strategy, it is recommended that ADHD students get positive comments or touches one hundred times a day. I know many teachers will say that's impossible and a little too much. The emphasis is on creating opportunities for positive rather than negative reinforcement. Teachers could set their cell phones to beep as a reminder to give positive attention to students. Teachers, modify behaviour in a variety of ways and settings. Use a combination of positive and negative reinforcement strategies, avoid punishments that erode self-esteem and hinders ADHD students from reaching their potential.

General Tips for Working with ADHD Children

Generally, a teacher should strive to be a good classroom manager. The teacher begins by trying to understand each student in the class. Teachers should question themselves, "What do I know about each student?" They should arm themselves with screening tools to help in making appropriate referrals if a behavioural problem is detected, in order to help distinguish between students with family issues, psychological problems, learning disorders, and/or attention-seeking and disruptive behaviours. Teachers may then be able to detect if the child fits a psychological profile that needs further investigation. The next step is to refer the child to a guidance counsellor. The teacher must remember that for every behaviour, there is a cause and a purpose. Teachers should become aware of his/her dialogue with students and avoid responding to a student based on how the behaviour is making the teacher feel personally.

At the start of the school year, teachers should teach students to accept differences to promote unity and a good class community. They should also teach students relaxation techniques and how to use these to calm down. Teachers should teach cooperative learning to help build community. Ultimately, teachers can teach students how to identify their feelings and how to control unwanted feelings.

In recent months, the Jamaican Ministry of Education has launched a program of positive disciplinary practices in schools. I truly endorse this approach. The concept of positive discipline is a disciplinary approach that avoids the use of punitive measures and emphasizes reinforcement of good behaviour while fading out bad behaviour. Teachers avoid verbally or physically abusing students. Schools using this approach help children feel that they have their best interest at heart so that they feel a sense of belonging and worthiness. This approach also promotes high levels of mutual respect, coupled with being encouraging and respectful. This is demonstrated by being firm but kind. Teachers take into consideration what the child is feeling, thinking, learning and their world view that could be promoting inappropriate behaviours. Teachers using alternative disciplinary measures make teaching social skills an important part of the curriculum. They also teach and exemplify skills of empathy, problem solving, and team building. As well, they identify students' strengths and use these strengths to empower and create a sense of positive experience for students.

The alternative positive disciplinary approach avoids the use of punishment and the removal of students from classrooms; limits the use of suspensions and disapproval statements; avoids using penalties that tend to be humiliating and disproportionate to the offences and avoids exclusion and flogging. The school avoids reliance on heavy security arrangements (security guards); locked doors; police presence in the school; and punitive discipline strategies that appear to aggravate, not reduce, vandalism, aggression, and disorder. In recent years, indications are that school personnel spend more time and energy in implementing punitive, rather than positive or preventive measures. We must agree that current punitive strategies do not work. School officials must minimize the use of punitive methods of control because reliance on reactive, punitive methods of control contributes to student antisocial behaviour. The use of positive behavioural reductive techniques should replace use of punitive methods, particularly for minor infractions. Positive reductive methods include modelling and various reinforcement strategies as outlined above.

A very important part of positive disciplinary measures is to begin by providing clear rules for student conduct and discipline. Engage students in setting both classroom and school-wide rules. This provides purpose and a sense of belonging. This helps with relationship building, which is a first step towards positive disciplining. Teachers should ensure that students' learning deficiencies are identified and addressed in well-structured remedial programmes. This will minimize behavioural problems associated with learning disabilities.

ACTIVITY: CASE EXAMPLES

The following cases exemplify situations that teachers may encounter in the classroom. Identify the possible problems students present with, in the scenarios illustrated below:

John is a twelve-year-old male who presents with the following behavioural symptoms:

- Eyes water and/or become red after a short time working,
- Complains of tired eyes; rubs eyes a lot,
- Puts head on desk to read,
- Oral reading is choppy: words skipped, endings left off, frequent repetitions,
- Loses place when reading,
- Talks loudly,
- Often asks you to repeat yourself,
- Comments about getting headaches after a short time working at reading or writing,
- Squints and peers close to see print,
- Peers at work on desk from an angle,
- Lifts eyes from page frequently to glance around,
- Closes one eye while reading or writing,
- Misunderstands you,
- Turns an ear towards you when you speak,
- Reading: The learner shows marked difficulty in oral and silent reading,
- Reading patterns are slow and deliberate,
- Skips words, re-reads lines in oral reading,
- May substitute, delete, add or transpose letters and syllables,
- Loses place on page,
- Avoids reading aloud,
- Reads words or syllables backwards; e.g., 'was' for 'saw', 'net' for 'ten',
- When reading silently, appears to be re-reading or reading very slowly (this can be attributable to poor visual processing),

- Cannot use basic phonics to sound out words,
- Reads with an overdependence on guessing and, as such, comprehension is compromised, evidenced in errors in answering questions related to the text,
- Reading style is halting and jerky,
- Expressive language: (writing, spelling)
- Is aggressive when called to do things on the board,
- Often leaves the class without permission.

Mary is a thirteen-year-old girl who came to the attention of the guidance counsellor because of disruptive behaviour. She displays the following behaviours:

- Is able to relate well to older or younger people, just not her peers,
- Displays good language skills,
- Tends to engage in out-of-seat behaviours, especially when near her teacher,
- Shouts across the classroom when she notices that the teacher is attending to other students,
- Is constantly sent out of class because she throws paper across the classroom,
- Appears aggressive.

Mr Brown, Matthew's teacher provided a description of Matthew's behaviour to the principal. He described Matthew's behaviour in the following way:

- "Matthew would always be hitting, pinching, or interfering with others. He darts out of the class. It is difficult for him to stay still. He would not sit at a table with other children. He would blurt out answers but often had the incorrect answers. He would not complete tasks. He may sit and begin to write in his book and by the time you look around, he is not there. He comes in again to find someone to play with, and then he is out of the class again. He is always disturbing other teachers' classes. He disturbs his other classmates. He walks around with a piece of stick and knocks the desk, then he goes outside again, provokes the children—basically, that kind of behaviour. When you are ready to start your class, this is when this child wants to sharpen a pencil, buy a book, and drink water. This is the time he will not give you the attention. He will be reading another book that we are not currently using. He gets up out of his seat when being seated is what is required. He will not pay attention. This could disrupt the class and valuable teaching time is lost. At the end of the session, the students have not grasped anything."

A teacher, in an interview with the school principal, gave a description of Paul's behaviour and articulates that Paul is a threat to other students:

- "This particular boy would beat up students. He would hit another child in the head. Every day, it is like a boxing ring in my class. This boy has beaten up a girl because he said the girl "dissed" him. The same student took a broom and hit another student in his head. It is not easy. He likes to be in charge. There was an incident with him recently. Another student told him some guy had taken something from his bag. He immediately went over to the guy, choked him, and slapped him in his face. The teacher continued his report that some boys were making a joke that this student used his hand and boxed a dog and the dog died. He comes to school and tells me all the illegal activities he engages in. When he commits illicit acts outside of school, he comes with the same rage to school. Many times these students end up in a power struggle, because they do not want the child's behaviour to affect other children. On the other hand, the teacher want respect from the child and the child wants to win the power struggle.

Mrs Hall is the form teacher for grade 10A and outlined her experience with two boys in her class:

- I have a student in my class who is partially deaf and has a learning problem. The boys I mentioned would interfere with the handicapped boy. They would tease and kick him. They would use their feet to trip him, and he would fall to the ground. The boy with behavioural issues would beat up students. He would pick on the quieter students. He would hit another child in the head. When the other child got up to retaliate, he would behave aggressively and say, "I will box you and kick you". This boy had beaten up a girl because he said the girl "dissed" him. The same boy took a broom and hit another student on his head. The child received stitches in his head because he received a huge cut on his forehead. There is another boy who has problems controlling his behaviour. When he comes to school, he walks out of class anytime. When the "devil kicks him" he will come back inside, kick whoever he wants to kick, box whoever he wants to box, and walks out again. The boy is very defiant. He goes outside of the classroom without my permission. He catches insects, takes off their tails and heads and throws them on the Grade One children. I said to him, 'Leave my class.' He said to me, 'I am not leaving, and you cannot take me out.' One day there was an incident at school and the same CD boy took up some stones and began throwing them at the teachers. The teachers had to run."

1. Outline the steps you would initiate with each of the students in the cases mentioned above.
2. Develop a behaviour modification programme to help each student.

CHAPTER 5

Self-Care: Stress Management for Life Management

Teaching is a very challenging job, and is even more challenging when dealing with children who have behavioural disorders. Having to cope with even one child in a classroom can be very stressful. I found that in my research on Jamaican schools, some teachers report having several students who present with characteristics of behavioural problems in their class. Having to deal with a number of students with behavioural problems on a daily and weekly basis can be very stressful.

Huberman (1993) speaks of the professional life cycle of teachers. He describes the first two to three years of teaching as career entry, often described as a phase of survival and discovery. Many of the teachers in my study concur with Huberman. They describe an entry period as a kind of culture shock, because they were not prepared to deal with students who have behavioural disorders. If this entry level is not successfully navigated, Huberman comments, about 25 per cent of beginning teachers leave the profession within the first five years of teaching because they do not reconcile the problems they face in dealing with students. He further comments that after the career entry phase, teachers usually enter a period of stabilisation characterized by increased self-confidence and pedagogical mastery. It is usually in this phase that the individual commits to becoming a dedicated teacher and sees teaching as a profession.

Teachers who remain in the profession after the first two to three years report that it is through good self-care that they are able to remain committed to the teaching process. They report of ensuring that they are knowledgeable about the students they will encounter in the teaching/learning process. They also report personal care including reading, exercising, spending time with family and friends, travelling or taking holidays, gardening, shopping, sewing/knitting/crocheting, spending time with pets and animals, going to church and becoming involved in church activities, playing sports, attending sporting events, eating out with friends, going to club events, going to the movies, and volunteering in their community or school. They stated that they separate themselves from work regularly. An underlying theme successful teachers underscore is that they do not take work home. They go to work and then leave it all at school for the next day.

Interventions the school system can take to prevent teacher burnout include the following:

1. Offer professional development activities, stress management workshops, relaxation training, time management workshops, nutrition, exercise and coping skills training.
2. Schools should ensure they improve working conditions for teachers. Included in this improved working condition would be to ensure a good classroom environment, and a good wage benefit.

Centring to Reduce Stress

In order to deal with personal and school stressors such as dealing with children with behavioural disorders, the teacher needs to be centred.

Centring is a state of mind that allows you to see every side of a situation that presents itself and to remain in that state of mind (that centre). It allows one to take actions that support their best well-being. Centring is fully and completely recognizing that life challenges are meant to be met head on and to be overcome. From the centre, the individual is able to see consequences, opportunities and non-opportunities. From a centred state of mind, the individual remains authentic, that is, an acknowledgment of the current situation. Authenticity does not sugar coat a situation; rather, it explores and sees the reality of the event. Authenticity is a prerequisite to centring; it is being true to yourself. Being authentic involves exploring the challenge and how this challenging situation makes you feel. It is getting in touch with your feelings and labelling them; identifying challenges in your frame of actuality and reality. Centring is that state of mind that achieves the highest value of acknowledgement. In doing this exploration, it shows you are at your centre.

Acknowledging the challenges, identifying feelings, and expressing feelings are the hallmarks of centring. At the centre, you have seen the left and right side of the situation. Inauthenticity can lead to developing a mental state of: anxiety, panic, obsessive-compulsive behaviour or depression, ultimately never regaining grounding—your centre. If you are a centred person, you have the advantage from the beginning of seeing both sides and taking realistic and practical actions that will ensure you are true to yourself and facing the reality from a centred state of mind. In centring, you gather all the possibilities, look at both sides, and bring the possibilities into the centre to create the balance in order to make authentic decisions.

The centred person takes full responsibility to stay centred, to face the future, because the possibilities are endless. One writer states, "We must return to solitude again and again if we hope to hear the voice of inspiration and if we want to live a fully realized life."

If you are a centred teacher, you will ensure that you take care of your spiritual needs and physical needs. Eat a balanced diet; get adequate sleep, which is essential; exercise regularly; and find time to laugh because it releases endorphins, the body's natural morphine. Work just enough for sustenance and covering. In a centred state of mind, teachers recognize that problems are a natural part of everyday life but will not allow themselves to be consumed by their challenges. You should surround yourself with positive people, be assertive, and make fun an integral part of your lives.

Stress Management Tips for Life Management

Teachers should recognize that managing stress is vital, and that stress management is the first priority in order to increase their effectiveness. Stress management begins with developing a close personal relationship with self—the centred self. The teacher should find time to be with self, practice self-talk—positive self-talk—to identify their strengths and make them an important part of who they are. As well, the teacher should identify weaknesses, and make a commitment to work on them to help relieve the anxieties associated with focusing on weaknesses.

It is very important, and often overlooked, to understand and take care of your inner child's needs. These unfulfilled needs can lead to frustration and dependence on others to satisfy those needs. You know yourself best and should strive to ensure that you meet your needs as they arise. Love yourself, nurture and take care of your physical, mental and spiritual self. Recognize that you are responsible for your happiness. Protect yourself from unhealthy situations and get up every day and count your blessings. Every day write down ten things you can give thanks for, and before going to bed, give thanks again. Use positive self-talk, positive affirmation and strive to become emotionally intelligent. Learn to care for your mind because you use it every second! Use mind calming exercises such as the 5-4-3-2-1 Activity—search the environment and find five things you see, four things you hear, three things you feel, two things you smell, and then say one good thing about yourself. This helps to calm the mind and reduces anxiety. Use guided visualisation wherein you imagine your favourite place—the sights, smells, and feelings that will invoke positive feelings after a hard day's work. This time is recovery time after a long day of dealing with stressful situations that confronted you during the day. Wind your day down with classical calming music that puts your mind at ease, because you deserve it.

Practice self-nourishment—it is recommended that everyone should include down time that is one hour per day, one day per week, and one week out of every twelve to sixteen weeks. You should also strive to get rest time—allow yourself to recreate and replenish your energy, and uplift your spirit. You should never feel drained after doing recreation. Relationships are an important part of stress reduction; enjoy other people and surround yourself with positive people. If you are the negative person, change it—this is to aid your own stress reduction. *Love yourself.*

Analyse your sleep habits and ensure that you get a good night's sleep. Go to bed and get up at a regular time. Develop a sleep ritual before bedtime; reduce noise; block out excess noise; purchase a quality mattress, turn yourself down during the last hour or two of the day. Avoid getting emotionally upset, and have a warm bath before going to bed.

There is a very good therapeutic technique—mindfulness—which means to make every moment in our lives meaningful and with purpose. Mindfulness is focusing your attention on the present moment—living in the here and now instead of the "what ifs" and "if onlys". The focus is on what is. Mindfulness Process is keeping the focus on the present and finding out what your purpose is in this moment, the moment you are in, the here and now. The mind might wander, and if it does, you should stop and observe. In this moment, where is your awareness or attention focused? Get in touch with what you are thinking, feeling, and sensing. Mindfulness is also about tuning in to what your body is experiencing, whether there is tension, tightness, and stress, or a feeling of accomplishment and achievement. Bring your awareness and attention back to the moment and your purpose by breathing in and breathing out. Do not attempt to change your breathing, but merely observe and experience the in-and-out of your breath and return to your purpose in the moment. This very powerful technique helps in refocusing and finding meaning and purpose in life.

Venting as a Stress Reduction Tool

The word venting may have a negative connotation but venting in a well-structured manner can relieve stress. It is a way to help in the centring process. A day full of frustrations from dealing with disruptive students, co-workers, and having to contend with daily stressors can take us from our centre and create stressful responses. Venting involves the following concepts of ventilating, emptying, needing, transformation, initiating, neutralizing, and growth.

Ventilating is the first step in venting wherein you talk through the current event or circumstances that is affecting you. This could be self-talk or talking to someone who will be able to listen carefully without judging.

The next step in the process involves the process of Emptying. In this sense, emptying is taking the time to get in touch with negative emotions tied to the event or circumstances causing the stress. You then name the emotions such as anger, hurt, frustration, confusion, hate, resentment, or malice. Getting in touch with your emotions creates an authentic feeling of being present with them. The process continues with you staying with the emotion in order to understand how the event or circumstances have affected you emotionally. It is time to ask yourself, *How am I feeling? What am I feeling because of thinking or talking about the situation?* Ask how useful this feeling has been for you. Has it affected your relationships, work or other areas of your life? Ask yourself, *How much longer do I want to feel this way?* Then make a decision as to what you want to do with these emotions. Emptying is releasing yourself of unwanted emotions, making a conscious decision that the emotion has served its purpose, and may be at this point, hindering you from engaging meaningfully in life. After emptying, there should be more clarity to your understanding of what you need to feel better.

In the next step, Needing, you try to identify what you need to change the feeling towards the event, cope with, or change the circumstances. A series of questions are useful in this stage. *If things are going to be different, what are my needs? How can I satisfy those needs?* Make a list of your needs and say how each need can be satisfied.

Transformation is the next step. *If I were to feel better and resolve the situation, what would that look like?* Create a picture or vision of what resolution would look like. For example, you could write: *I would be better informed as to how to deal with children with disruptive behaviour.* Or: *I will practice better classroom management or set aside a stress free day.* These are just a few examples.

The step of Initiating within the venting process addresses what steps you now take to effect the change or transformation. This is the actual "doing stage", wherein practical steps are taken to ensure that the situation causing stress is dealt with and the situation is resolved.

This leads to the next step, Neutralizing. The issues may not all together be resolved immediately or short term, but the question is,

How do I continue to function without all the negative emotions that come with this situation? Neutralizing involves compromise, accepting the things that cannot change, learning how to empathize, learning forgiveness to facilitate healing and letting go. Learn positive self-talk and use of affirmations. Use of positive self-talk helps to neutralize persistent negative feelings, and creates good mental well-being. Use of affirmations confirms that you are only human trying to exist in a troublesome world, but you are a survivor with qualities that will make you rebound.

Following the above steps will ultimately lead to growth. One of our fundamental rights is to grow and change. The purpose is to learn fundamental lessons from every situation we encounter in life; to look at where we were and where we are now; to be wiser and smarter after every situation, so we become more in touch with the meaning and purpose of life. Venting is a process of healing and continually retooling to reduce anxiety and depression and promote good mental well-being.

Teachers must take good care of themselves in order to navigate the ever-challenging school environment. This is even more so when you are teaching disruptive children. If your stress on a daily basis is overwhelming because you are not coping, teaching may not be for you. If this is so, you will want to exit the profession or teach adults, if you are qualified to do so. For those who teach children with disruptive behaviour disorders on a daily basis, stress management should be a way of life.

Outline Your Stress Reduction Plan

1. Reducing stress is important to me because _____.
2. Making a commitment to myself to create and follow my stress management plan will help me in the following ways _____.
3. A major source of stress in my life is _____.

4. Some things I can do that would help me feel better are _____.

5. Two things I can do today to help my stress level are _____.

6. Taking care of myself is important and will help me in the following ways _____.

7. Some ways I could take care of myself are_____.

8. Of these things listed above, the thing I would most like to try and will stick with is _____.

9. I expect that not everyone will support my efforts to reduce stress in my life, and when this happens, some things I can do to stay with my plan are _____.

<www.mindtools.com/rs/StressDiary. For tips about reducing stress, visit http://www.mindtools.com/smpage.html>.

Conclusion

The purpose of this book is to bring into sharp awareness the fact that children who present disruptive behavioural patterns may be experiencing a psychological disorder. This knowledge would then alert teachers to the need to ensure that the right procedure is followed in getting help for students with disruptive behaviours. To begin with, the child is sent to a guidance counsellor for screening, the guidance counsellor in turn, consults with parents and the appropriate referral can be made to a psychologist or psychiatrist for evaluation. If the child's diagnosis is positive for a disruptive behaviour disorder, then all parties concerned need to arrange to meet in order to put appropriate strategies in place to facilitate treatment. The teachers about whom this book is primarily concerned will come from a place of understanding. They will develop appropriate behaviour modification strategies that will help in allowing the child to reach his/her potential despite their problem. The teacher will also ensure that in caring for others' educational needs, they care for themselves in the process. The teacher's awareness that there is a biological basis for disruptive behaviours disallows the assignation of blame to poor environment, but assists in gaining an understanding before forming conclusions. Teachers should also be aware of strategies that they can use to ensure that disruptive students reach their potential. Teachers are aware of the importance of self-reflection and teaching self-monitoring as an integral part of helping disruptive students.

I am hoping that if I should, in the future, replicate the study on Jamaican teachers' knowledge and understanding of the disruptive disorders that it would find them to be very knowledgeable about the disorders.

REFERENCES

Albert, L. (1989). *A teacher's guide to cooperative discipline: How to manage your classroom and promote self-esteem.* PA: American Guidance Service. American Psychiatric Association. (2000). *Diagnostic and statistical manual of mental disorders* (4th ed., text revision). Washington, DC: Author.

Beebe-Frankenberger, M., Lane, K. L., Bocian, K. M., Gresham, F. M., & MacMillan, D. L. (2005). Students with or at risk for problem behaviour: Betwixt and between teacher and parent expectations. *Preventing School Failure, 49,* 10–17.

Bekle, B. (2004). Knowledge and attitude about attention deficit hyperactivity disorder (ADHD): A comparison between practicing teachers and undergraduate education students. *Journal of Attention Deficit Disorder, 7*(3), 151–61.

Cheney, D., Osher, T., & Caesar, M. (2002). Providing ongoing skill development and support for educators and parents of students with emotional and behavioral disabilities. *Journal of Child and Family Studies, 11,* 79–89.

Cipkala-Gaffin, J. (1998). A diagnosis and treatment of attention–deficit/ hyperactivity disorder [Electronic version]. *Perspectives in Psychiatric Care, 34,* 18. Corrie, L. (1997). The interaction between teachers' knowledge and skills when managing troublesome classroom behaviour. *Cambridge Journal of Education, 27,* 93–105.

Evans, I. (2001). *Inside Jamaican schools.* Kingston, Jamaica: University of the West Indies Press.

Farmer, T. W. (2000). The social dynamics of aggressive and disruptive behaviour in school: Implications for behaviour consultation. *Journal of Educational and Psychological Consultation, 11,* 299–321.

Fornarotto, S., & O'Connell, C. B. (2002). Managing ADHD and comorbid ODD and CD. *Physician Assistant,* 20–31.

Frolich, J., Dopfner, M., Biegert H., & Lehmkuhl, G. (2002). General practice of pedagogic management by teachers of Hyperkinetic Attention Deficit disordered children in the classroom. *Journal of Prax Kinderpsychology, Kinderpsychiatric, 51,* 494–506

Gable, R. A. (2004). Hard times and an uncertain future: Issues that confront the field of emotional/behavioural disorders. *Education and Treatment of Children, 27,* 341–352.

Greene, R. W., Beszterczey, S. K., Katzenstein, T., Park, K., & Goring, J. (2002). Are students with ADHD more stressful to teach? *Journal of Emotional and Behavioural Disorders, 10,* 79–89.

Hickling, F. (1994). *Violence in Jamaica*. Kingston, Jamaica: University of the West Indies, Institute of Social and Economic Research.

Huberman, M.A., (1993). The lives of teachers. NY: Teachers College Press.

Jamaican Ministry of Education Youth & Culture. (2004). *The program for alternative student support 2004*. Jamaica: Author.

Jenson, W. R., Olympia, D., Farley, M., & Clark, E. (2004). Positive psychology and externalizing students in a sea of negativity. *Psychology in the Schools, 41,* 67–79.

Jerome, L., Gordon, M., & Hustler, P. (1994). A comparison of American and Canadian teachers' knowledge and attitudes towards Attention Deficit Hyperactivity Disorder (ADHD). *Canadian Journal of Psychiatry, 9,* 563–7.

Kokkinos, C. M., Panayiotou, G., & Davazoglou, A. M. (2004). Perceived seriousness of pupils' undesirable behaviours: The student teachers' perspective. *Educational Psychology, 24,* 109–120.

Lane, K. L., Pierson, M. R., & Givner, C. C. (2003). Teacher expectations of student behaviour: Which skills do elementary and secondary teachers deem necessary for success in the classroom? *Education and Treatment of Children, 26,* 413–430.

Lane, K. L., Wehby, J., & Barton-Arwood, S. M. (2005). Students with and at risk for emotional and behavioral disorders: Meeting their social and academic needs. *Preventing School Failure, 49*(2), 6–9.

Madaan, V, (2008). Assessing the efficacy of treatments for ADHD: Overview of methods logical issues. CNS Drugs, 22(4) 275–290.

National Institute of Mental Health (NIMH) (2009). ADHD medication treatment associated with higher academic performance in elementary School. Retrieved May 6, 2009 from www.nimh.org.

Palardy, J. M., & Palardy, T. J. (1987). Classroom discipline: Prevention and intervention strategies. *Education, 108,* 87–92.

Pisecco, S., Huzinec, C., & Curtis, D. (2001). The effect of child characteristics on teachers' acceptability of classroom-based behavioral strategies and psychostimulant medication for the treatment of ADHD. *Journal of Clinical Child Psychology, 30,* 413–421.

Pottinger, A. (2001). Incidence and treatment of attention deficit in the Jamaican context Daily Gleaner,

Poulou, M., & Norwich, B. (2000). Teachers' perceptions of students with emotional and behavioural difficulties: Severity and prevalence. *European Journal of Special Needs Education, 15,* 171–187.

Reis, E. M. (2002). Attention deficit hyperactivity disorder: Implications for the classroom teacher. *Journal of Instructional Psychology, 29,* 175–178.

Richardson, B. G., & Shupe, M. J. (2003,). The importance of teacher self-awareness in working with students with emotional and behavioural disorders. *Teaching Exceptional Children,* 8–13.

Robin, L. N. (1974). *Deviant children grown up: A sociological study of sociopathic personality.* Huntington NY: Krieger.

Sciutto, M. J., Nolfi, C. J., & Bluhm, C. (2004). Effects of child gender and symptom type on referrals for ADHD by elementary school teachers. *Journal of Emotional and Behavioural Disorders, 12,* 247–253.

Sciutto, M. J., Terjesen, M. D., & Bender Frank, A. S. (2000). Teachers' knowledge and misperceptions of attention–deficit/hyperactivity disorder. *Psychology in the Schools, 37,* 115–122.

Semmler, M. (2001). *ADHD: How can teachers counter the effect in the classroom?* Retrieved [July 7, 2005, from http://www.thecoo. edu/~masemm/adhd_research_paper.htm?

Smith, D. E., & Muenchen, R. A. (1995). Gender and age variations in the self-image of Jamaican adolescents. *Adolescence, 30,* 643–654.

Stevens, J., Quittner, A. L., & Abikoff, H. (1998). Factors influencing elementary school teachers' ratings of ADHD and ODD behaviours. *Journal of Clinical Child Psychiatry, 27,* 406–414.

Sutherland, K. S. (2000). Prompting positive interactions between teachers and students with emotional/behavioural disorders. *Preventing School Failure, 44*(3), 110–115.

Tyler, K., & Jones, B. D. (2002, June). Teachers' responses to the ecosystemic approach to changing chronic problem behaviour in schools. *Pastoral Care,* 30–39.

Vereb, R. L., & DiPerna, J. C. (2004). Teachers' knowledge of ADHD, treatments for ADHD, and treatment acceptability: An initial investigation. *School Psychology Review, 33,* 421–428.

Voeller, K. K. S. (2004). Attention-deficit hyperactivity disorder (ADHD). *Journal of Child Neurology, 19,* 798–814.

Weiner, L. (2003). Why is classroom management so vexing to urban teachers? *Theory into Practice, 42,* 305–312.

Wickman, K. (1928). Children's behavior and teachers' attitudes. NY: The Commonwealth Fund, Division of Publications, Psychoanal. Rev., 16:454-456.

Wingenfeld, S. A. (2002). Assessment of behavioural and emotional difficulties in children and adolescents. *Peabody Journal of Education, 77,* 85–105.

ABOUT THE AUTHOR

Dr Bell is a clinical psychologist specializing in child, adolescent, and adult interventions. She employs a variety of therapeutic modalities for clinical disorders such as depression, anxiety and schizophrenia. Dr Bell taught at both the secondary and tertiary levels of education for the past thirty-three years. Dr Bell has been a motivational speaker, educator, author, and columnist who strives for excellence in whatever projects she undertakes. She was awarded the Jamaica Tourist Board Teacher's Award for Outstanding Project Implementation in the field of tourism development, The Jamaica Social Workers Association Prize, and The Council for the Voluntary Social Services Prize for Academic Excellence, at the University of the West Indies. Dr Bell has made significant contributions to psychology and is a pioneer in this field in Western Jamaica. She is sought after to provide psychological perspective on many issues affecting the Jamaican psyche, frequently quoted in the news media, and is highly respected for her contribution to the field of psychology. She has published a book entitled *Word Once Unspoken*—a book of therapeutic poems, which she uses as part of poetry therapy for clients.

REVIEW BY DANIEL ECKSTEIN, PH.D.

Dr Bell has created a timely contribution relative to the challenges for teachers regarding ADHD behavioural classroom disruptions. The book features a skilful blending of her own clinical experiences with students, coupled with qualitative research based on classroom teachers' experiences along with timely and relevant supportive research by other experts in the field as well. There are specific helpful sections on such topics such as the use of psychotropic medications, as well as concrete recommended strategies like reframing and behaviour modification. The final chapter on self-care is also filled with excellent suggestions for teachers in helping reduce the amount of stress relative to such challenging students.

Daniel Eckstein, Ph.D., Professor of Behavioural Sciences and Course Director, Medical Ethics, Saba University School of Medicine, Saba, National Dutch Caribbean, and author of several books including *Leadership by Encouragement*

ABOUT THE BOOK

This book, *A Teacher's Guide to Understanding the Disruptive Behaviour Disorders*, is designed to help teachers who are confronted with disruptive behaviours in their classroom. Teachers often complain of being unprepared to deal with disruptive behaviours. They experience frustration when they are unable to carry out the teaching/learning process in an effective manner as a result of disruptive behaviours. This book seeks to guide teachers in how to understand and deal effectively with disruptive behaviours in the classroom. This knowledge will help to relieve the stress and frustration often experienced when they have to deal with disruptive students.